A Year of Picnics

ALSO BY ASHLEY ENGLISH

Handmade Gatherings: Recipes and Crafts for Seasonal Celebrations and Potluck Parties

Quench: Handcrafted Beverages to Satisfy Every Taste and Occasion

A Year of Picnics

*Recipes for Dining Well
in the Great Outdoors*

Ashley English

PHOTOGRAPHS BY Jen Altman

ROOST BOOKS

BOULDER

2017

ROOST BOOKS

An imprint of Shambhala Publications, Inc.

4720 Walnut Street

Boulder, Colorado 80301

roostbooks.com

9 8 7 6 5 4 3 2 1

First Edition

Printed in China

♾ This edition is printed on acid-free paper that meets the American National Standards Institute Z39.48 Standard.

♻ Shambhala Publications makes every effort to print on recycled paper. For more information please visit www.shambhala.com.

Distributed in the United States by Penguin Random House LLC and in Canada by Random House of Canada Ltd

Designed by **CAT GRISHAVER**

Library of Congress Cataloging-in-Publication Data

Names: English, Ashley, 1976–
Title: A year of picnics: recipes for dining well in the great outdoors / Ashley English;
photographs by Jen Altman.
Description: First Edition. | Boulder: Roost, 2017. | Includes index.
Identifiers: LCCN 2015003041 | ISBN 9781611802153 (hardcover: alk. paper)
Subjects: LCSH: Picnics. | Outdoor cooking. | LCGFT: Cookbooks.
Classification: LCC TX823 .E54 2017
| DDC 642/.3—dc23 LC record available at https://lccn.loc.gov/2015003041

»» contents

»introduction

*E*very year, right around mid–March, I start to get a profound craving. This desire of mine is intense. I pine for it, long for it, desire it so fervently that it feels I could almost conjure it into reality, if I just thought hard enough. What quickens my senses and heightens my emotions, as the chill of winter begins to fade and the daffodils push their canary-colored bonnets up through the soil, is the prospect of eating outdoors. Just before the first official beginning of spring, a sunny, cloudless day will appear and, with it, a shift in temperature accommodating enough for me to turn to my husband and say, "You want to eat on the patio tonight?" or, better yet, "Let's go on a picnic!"

For as long as humans have lived, they have picnicked. This has manifested in various ways throughout the ages, from the simple meals of bread and sheep's milk cheese of traveling shepherds to the elaborate outdoor feasts of wealthy Victorians. Sure, there are the challenges of weather and insects to consider. There's also the perishable nature of certain foods to bear in mind. Above those possible derailments, though, is the sheer, ineffable joy experienced when sitting down at a table or on a blanket, taking in the scenery, and enjoying a meal— whether humble or grandiose—outside.

This book offers twenty ideas for creative, handmade picnics. Every outing is themed, and you'll find recipes and activity suggestions specific to each picnic. Each picnic is also tethered, in both concept and menu, to a particular location. Ultimately, what that means is that what is done and what is consumed at these twenty picnics refer back to their setting. From a pasta dish meant to mimic a bird's nest at the Bird Watching Picnic to reading tea leaves and playing cards at the Afternoon Tea Picnic, from S'mores Brownies enjoyed at the Winter Picnic to crafting an actual table for carrying along to the Table to Farm Picnic, the food and the festivities invoke the spirit of the place that inspired them.

Whether you re-create every picnic and cook every recipe or not, my hope is that you will come away from this book inspired. I have long felt that we become better stewards of our planet, with an increased desire to take care of our environment, when we spend time out in nature. The more you're around something you enjoy, something that brings you happiness, the more inclined you are to want to care for and nurture it. Sure, these are just picnics, but they can be so very much more than that, really. They can serve as experiences that compel us to be mindful of our actions in this place we all call home. The fact that you'll be eating delicious foods and enjoying stimulating activities, all in a lovely setting, only sweetens the deal.

Happy picnicking!

»picnic essentials

At first consideration, it would seem that all one needs to pull off a glorious picnic are some tasty eats, a beautiful setting, and a comfy blanket. On many levels, that's completely true. There are several aspects to picnicking, however, that when mindfully attended to in advance ensure an even more spectacular occasion.

✳ LOCATION & WEATHER

CHOOSING A SITE

My idea in creating this book was to develop a series of highly site-specific picnicking concepts. What that means is that the foods, beverages, and activities all speak to the location of the picnic itself. So, for picnicking beside a Sacred Tree (see page 87), the recipes all speak to foods sourced from trees, or for a High-Altitude Picnic (page 159), the menu consists of foods appropriate for consuming in such a setting. Careful consideration of your picnicking site can go far toward creating a pleasant experience. Not only should it be pretty, but also the foods served and the equipment and servingware utilized should all relate to it. An elaborate Afternoon Tea Picnic (page 107) might not be the best choice on a sandy beach, while a Rooftop Picnic (page 189) begs for foods that are easily transportable. Paying attention to the specific needs of your intended site and using them as your starting point in planning will go far toward creating a great time for all.

CHECKING THE WEATHER

As the duo Outkast wisely rapped, "You can plan a pretty picnic, but you can't predict the weather." While working on this book, a good number of photo shoots had to be rescheduled or moved to later times of the day owing to inclement weather. While snowfall is just what you might want for a stunning Winter Picnic (page 225), a torrential downpour or continuous rain isn't an ideal picnicking situation. Check the weather five days before your intended picnic, then again two days beforehand. If the forecast calls for a 70 percent or greater likelihood of poor weather conditions, you might want to look for another day. For last-minute picnics, check the forecast before packing the picnic basket, as storms can roll in fast, even when the skies are cloudless and blue at present.

BACKUP PLANS

I have long been a devout disciple of the religion of preparation. Need some dental floss? I've got it in my purse. Have a headache? I've got something for that, too, also in my purse. Ditto a knife, matches, mini scissors, bandages, snacks, a dictionary, and more. I was this way before I had a child, and now I'm even more so. How does this apply to picnics? Be prepared, friends. While rain might not be in the forecast, if you live in an area with variable weather conditions (like I do), a summer shower could sneak up out of nowhere. While you don't necessarily need to slog in every item you might possibly need, it's a good idea to bring along a sweater or umbrella if you anticipate a turn in weather. Same with a roll of paper towels and a spare old bath towel, for drying off damp spaces you wish to picnic on or around. Like I always say, better to not need it and have it than to need it and not have it.

FOOTWEAR AND CLOTHING

After you've determined your picnic location, make your footwear selection accordingly. If you're hiking up a mountain, you'll want sturdy ankle support, as you'll be carrying your food and gear uphill, which could possibly throw off your balance a bit. If you're on a creek bank, opt for footwear that can handle getting wet while providing a bit of traction to prevent slipping. The same consideration should be given to clothing selection. Keep the particulars of the terrain you're visiting in mind when getting dressed. If you've got a bit of a walk to your location, perhaps a long garment that drags a bit on the ground might not be ideal. If your setting is a bit wild and natural, your beloved cashmere sweater that could get caught on wild brambles might best be left at home.

WEIGHT OF OBJECTS

The serving vessels and servingware you select for your picnic should also be based on the location. If you've got an upward climb ahead of you, then you want to leave the ceramics at home and opt for lightweight metal instead. If it's a short walk from your vehicle to the picnicking site, though, select objects you think will enhance the overall look of the meal. At a Table to Farm Picnic—if it isn't much of a walk to where you plan to feast—a lovely ceramic bowl could be just the thing to serve gazpacho in (page 45).

LENGTH OF TRANSIT

Baskets, blankets, food—it can really add up in terms of weight. If you've got lots of picnic participants willing to schlep, fantastic! If not, however, you might want to consider bringing along a wagon for transporting goods from your vehicle to the site. This is a great option for level spaces.

✷ EQUIPMENT & EXTRAS

PICNIC BASKETS

Options abound when choosing what to transport your food and servingware in. The iconic picnic basket is a thing of beauty. With a handle for easy transport and a flat surface that can be appropriated as a tabletop, picnic baskets are easily found. Antiques stores and online sites such as Etsy are wonderful resources to scour, both for vintage and for new offerings. Think outside the basket, too, with vintage suitcases, which also have handles and flat surfaces. Wooden crates are fantastic options for carrying heavier items, while backpacks are just the thing for locations that are a bit of a walk to get to or require an uphill climb to access.

BLANKETS

For me, picnicking is more than simply the act of eating outdoors. This is what picnics are about at their most basic, it's true. More than that, though, they're occasions for appreciating beauty and life in natural settings. To that end, I like to do as much as I can to make the picnic itself beautiful too. The blanket is the foundation for the scene. Actually, I use "blanket" a bit loosely, as I've also employed rugs and tablecloths on many a picnic. Some blankets are expressly made for picnicking, with sewn-in weatherproof backings for keeping them dry (this can also be done at home—many online tutorials are available). I've even brought along "bolstering" or "support" rugs, to be put down on damp or uneven surfaces, such as those found alongside creeks or in dense forests, and then topped them with blankets. Tablecloths are also nice options to consider, especially when picnicking in areas with lush, thick grass.

ENAMELWARE

Picnicking and enamelware were made for each other. Lightweight and highly durable, enamelware will stand the test of time. Many vintage options can be sourced at antiques and thrift stores, as well as online from sites such as Etsy or eBay, while new options are from outdoor-living suppliers as well as online. There's an enamelware option available in pretty much every color palette, too, so you can match your servingware to the setting and occasion, if that's of interest to you (it is to me!).

STAINLESS STEEL *(lightweight)*

If you happen to be out thrifting or visiting yard sales and see some small metal bowls, metal cups, or metal plates of any size, grab them. Lightweight stainless steel is a fantastic option for picnicking, whether for storing and transporting food in or for serving it on. It can withstand getting knocked around in transit and always looks good.

WOOD

If you were to visit my home, you'd see that wood plays a huge role. Not only are all the floors wood, but the kitchen countertops and cabinets are made of wood, the walls throughout are covered in wooden beadboard, and the couch, dining room table, and beds are all wood (as is most of the furniture, including the dining chairs and armchairs). We also heat our home with a large woodstove. It stands to reason, then, that we would use a good deal of wooden vessels and utensils in cooking and serving. On picnics, wood is lightweight, lovely to look at, and durable (remember to wash it by hand, though, as wooden objects can't withstand electric dishwashing). Wooden bowls, plates, and even flatware are highly recommended as you build up your picnicking arsenal.

LIDDED JARS

I'm not a big fan of plastic. Not only does it take finite, precious fossil fuels to create, but also, to me, it's simply unattractive. To that end, I'm always on the hunt for durable storage containers made of alternative materials, such as glass and metal. Lidded jars are perfect for both storing and transporting food in, as well as eating out of (see the Dried Cherry Granola and Ambrosia Parfaits on page 25 and the Mason Jar Apple Cardamom Crumbles on page 187).

COMPOSTABLE DINNERWARE

In the past few years, a number of companies have begun manufacturing compostable dinnerware. From wooden utensils to bamboo and potato-based plates and bowls, it's now easier than ever to obtain attractive, biodegradable servingware for your picnicking needs. When you're done, simply toss the items into your compost bin and let nature take its course!

CLOTH NAPKINS

In an attempt at cutting down on waste, I use cloth napkins in my home. When out picnicking, I do the same. Not only can cloth napkins be used again and again, they don't tear like paper napkins do. That said, if you do opt for paper napkins or paper towels, consider adding them to the compost afterward.

KEEPING FOODS HOT

There are several ways of serving food warm at a picnic. If your house-to-site distance isn't that far, and you wish to serve something like a hot soup or stew, you can simply bring your dish to a simmer right before leaving and then serve it within one hour. Otherwise, you can transport it in a wide-mouth thermos, zip it into an insulated container intended for keeping foods hot, or place it in a cooler lined on the bottom with towels and/or kitchen cloths. If using the last option, cover the hot container with towels after placing it in the cloth-lined cooler, because open airspace will quickly dissipate heat. Beverages stored in thermoses will stay warm for hours.

KEEPING FOODS COLD

Insulated coolers are ubiquitous sights at picnics, and for good reason. They work expertly at keeping foods and beverages cold. After preparing any foods you intend to serve cold, allow them to cool to room temperature and then store in the refrigerator. Then, when you're ready to head out for your picnic, pack ice into the bottom of the cooler and set the food containers on top. To make ice last even longer, first place a bag of dry ice on the bottom of the cooler, cover it over with ice, and then place the food on top. Keep the cooler lid closed whenever not in use, and store the cooler in a shady location at your picnicking destination. When you return home, if there is any ice left in your cooler, you can consider your leftover items safe to consume (assuming they were stored in the cooler the whole time); if the ice is all melted (and you didn't use dry ice), the food isn't safe to eat. Reusable ice packs are also especially nice to use, as they avoid the need to purchase new bags of ice each time. You can make homemade ice packs, too, by simply filling empty milk jugs with water and freezing them.

KEEPING FOODS FROZEN

Frozen foods at a picnic? Is that even possible? Indeed, it is! With a bit of dry ice, you can bring along a frozen treat, such as the Mango Lassi Ice Pops (page 67), to enjoy on your picnic. Readily available at grocery stores in a separate bin adjacent to the frozen aisle, dry ice will keep frozen goods frozen for up to twenty-four hours. It can't be touched with bare skin, though, so be sure to wear gloves when handling it, or keep it wrapped in plastic (most dry ice comes in plastic bags anyway—just be sure not to touch any that might have escaped from the bag). Place the dry ice on top of any foods you wish to remain frozen.

TRASH AND COMPOST BAGS

By utilizing reusable servingware and dinnerware, I'm able to keep trash generated at picnics to a minimum. Typically what remains can be recycled or composted. To that end, I often bring along a paper bag to store compostable matter in and a receptacle for holding recyclables (or I just store them back in the picnic basket, to be sorted later at home). Whatever you elect to do, keep in mind you'll need to bring something to transport waste in.

BUG SPRAY

Bringing along a bottle of bug spray is essential. You may have found the perfect setting and have brought along the most delicious meal, only to have all your efforts foiled by stinging winged creatures. Pick up a bottle and have it always at the ready, or better yet, make your own.

✳ all-natural bug spray

You've put so much thought into the location, food, and activities, the last thing you want is to have your planning outdone by stinging, biting insects. This easy-to-make spray will help keep them at bay.

YOU WILL NEED

1 cup of grain alcohol

Vodka or witch hazel (see Note)

10 drops citronella essential oil

7 drops lavender essential oil

7 drops rose geranium
   essential oil

6 drops rosemary essential oil

TO MAKE

1. Place all the ingredients into a spray bottle (I prefer metal misters around 11–12 ounces in size). Shake well. Spray liberally over any exposed skin either before venturing outdoors or as soon as you arrive at your destination. Reapply if you get wet or are sweating heavily.

Note: You'll need enough vodka or witch hazel to fill the bottle after the grain alcohol is added; the amount will vary based on the volume of your bottle.

spring AND summer

» breakfast «

PICNIC

Every morning, nearly without fail, I wake up ravenous. No matter how much food I consumed the evening before, and regardless of the hour at which I consumed it, come dawn's early light, my stomach is empty and growling and in need of some edibles, stat. Fortunately, I always wake up, well, "awake." Which is to say, I wake up ready to go. Pumped. Jazzed. Prepared to greet the day. I received this inclination genetically, from my father. Also a morning dove, he gets out of bed, slides on his slippers, and saddles up to life with gusto and gumption.

However, I recognize that not everyone wakes up in the same mood. Some are perhaps a bit disgruntled or disoriented until they have their morning coffee or morning run or other similarly invigorating routine. My husband, Glenn, is such a person. Don't ask him anything important for at least an hour after he wakes up. Different people wake up differently. Which is why the idea of a morning picnic is so good. Whether you rise and shine or need a bit of "polishing" before you're ready for prime time, a breakfast picnic will accommodate the needs of you and everyone else.

The foods, beverage, and activities included in this picnic are geared toward waking you up in a manner that is pleasing to all the senses. Tastes, sights, textures, and scents are all employed. There are also two suggestions for using laughter as a means of getting you going in the morning. Jokes and goofy games geared toward producing a sincere chuckle or even a robust guffaw will help get blood pumping and bodies moving.

I'd never gone on a breakfast picnic before I attended the one I hosted. It was a seemingly obvious, fantastic idea that had never before occurred to me (or anyone else I know, for that matter). As we sat on huge rocks in Reed Creek, which flows through the Asheville Botanical Gardens, the sights and sounds and silly antics were beyond welcoming, and entirely enlivening. My first breakfast picnic was far from my last, and I hope the same will hold true for you and your fellow picnickers.

✳ to MAKE & DO

SELECT A SITE

For a morning picnic, I suggest choosing a site that's easy to access at a location that's not terribly cumbersome to reach. You and your guests are still likely waking up a bit, so picnicking in a site with plenty of parking (or bike racks!) and clearly appointed walking paths would be ideal. If you're particularly ambitious, a location where your guests could view the sunrise would be especially epic!

PLAY GAMES

It's the morning, and unless you're the "roll out of bed rarin' to go" type, you and your guests might still be a bit groggy. Get your blood flowing and your heart pumping by playing games. Whether something active like Hide and Seek or more cerebral like Twenty Questions, games are a surefire means of getting you going.

Eight Emotions is a theater improv game I learned in high school. It's designed to help budding actors work on character development and adaptability. No matter whom I'm playing it with, it always, always elicits loads of laughs, and will most definitely wake everyone up.

To play, choose two people to be the actors. Briefly send them out of earshot while you and the other guests create their "characters." The more embellished the characters, the funnier. Accents are particularly sure to gain laughs. Think "nun from Brooklyn" or "firefighter from Boston" or "farmer from Scotland." Then come up with a list of eight emotions. These can include everything from envy to rage to lust to less obvious emotional states, like "reaction to an overflowing toilet."

Call your actors back over, and assign them each one of the characters you've created. Then give them the first emotion. While remaining in character, have the two interact with each other, in the given emotion. Once they seem to really be going with that emotion, switch to the next. Continue on, switching emotions as the two actors interact in character with each other, until you've named all eight emotions.

TELL JOKES

I do so love a good joke. Whether of the type to amuse young children or of the more bawdy persuasion, jokes and laughter undeniably wake up our bodies and our minds. When inviting guests to join you, ask them to come prepared with a joke. It needn't be long or involved, only funny (if even only to the joke teller!). Share your jokes and watch as the laughter flows and the slumber departs.

✳ *to* BEHOLD & EXPLORE

SIGHTS AND SOUNDS

Sensory stimulation is a wonderful means of waking up. Your taste buds and olfactory organs will be engaged with the meal, so give yourself an opportunity to explore sights, sounds, and textures, too. In whatever locale you've chosen for your breakfast picnic, see if there might be a bright, vivid wildflower or tree to observe. Listen closely, observing whatever sounds filter in. Find a rock or stone or patch of grass or any other texture to explore. In no time, last night's sleep will fade into distant memory.

››› Smoky Chai

The smoky fragrance of this tea will wake you up even before the liquid makes its way to your lips. Cradling a mug of it in your hands, especially should the morning be on the chilly side, will expedite the wake-up process, too. It's also just plain delicious. SERVES 4

YOU WILL NEED

4 cups cold water

6 cardamom pods (see Note)

6 whole cloves

6 black peppercorns

2 tablespoons coarsely chopped fresh ginger

1 tablespoon plus 1 teaspoon loose Lapsang souchong tea or 3 tea bags

2 tablespoons honey (or to your preferred sweetness)

½ cup whole milk

TO MAKE

1. Add the water, cardamom, cloves, peppercorns, and ginger to a medium saucepan. Bring to a boil over high heat.

2. Reduce the heat to low, place the tea in a tea strainer if using loose tea and add to the pan (otherwise, add the tea bags), along with the honey and milk. Whisk to combine, and simmer for 5 minutes.

3. Remove the pan from the heat. Cover and steep for 5 minutes longer.

4. Remove the tea; set aside to compost. I like to leave the spices in, but you can discard them if you prefer.

Note: Bruise your cardamom pods before adding them to the water by hitting them with the back of a spoon. ‹‹‹

»» Cardamom, Rose Water, *and* Berry Coffee Cake

There are several ingredients that, when I see them in a recipe or on a menu, I know almost without question that I will like the dish. Cardamom and rose water are two such flavor luminaries. Here I have incorporated them into a coffee cake, riddled it with berries throughout, and covered it all with a nutty pistachio and walnut topping. This coffee cake is guaranteed to make you wake up happy.

MAKES ONE 9-INCH CAKE

YOU WILL NEED

for the streusel topping

½ cup roasted and salted
   pistachios, chopped

½ cup chopped roasted
   walnut pieces

¼ cup unbleached
   all-purpose flour

¼ cup packed light brown sugar

2 tablespoons unsalted butter,
   cold

2½ teaspoons ground cardamom

¼ teaspoon sea salt

for the coffee cake

½ cup (1 stick) unsalted butter,
   melted

½ cup packed light brown sugar

½ cup granulated sugar

2 large eggs

2 teaspoons vanilla extract

2 cups all-purpose flour

1 teaspoon baking powder

1 teaspoon baking soda

¼ teaspoon sea salt

1 cup whole milk yogurt

2 teaspoons rose water

2 cups fresh or frozen berries, such
   as raspberries or blackberries

TO MAKE

1. Preheat the oven to 350°F. Lightly butter a 9-inch springform pan and set aside.

2. *Prepare the Streusel Topping:* Put all the ingredients for the streusel into a food processor. Pulse just until the butter is incorporated and the nuts are finely minced. If mixing by hand, combine all the ingredients except the nuts in a medium bowl, crumbling them together with a pastry cutter or two forks. Chop the nuts and stir in. Set the mixture aside.

3. *Prepare the Coffee Cake:* In a large bowl, beat together the melted butter, sugars, eggs, and vanilla with an electric mixer until smooth and somewhat fluffy, 2 to 3 minutes.

4. In a medium bowl, sift together the flour, baking powder, baking soda, and salt. In a small bowl, whisk together the yogurt and rose water. Add the flour mixture to the creamed butter mixture alternately with the yogurt and rose water, beginning and ending with the flour mixture. Beat until just smooth after each addition.

5. Stir in the berries. Pour the batter into the prepared pan and spread the streusel on top.

6. Bake for 60 to 75 minutes, until the topping is golden brown and a knife or skewer poked into the center of the cake comes out clean (the center should not jiggle). Let cool for 10 minutes, then remove the sides of the pan. Allow to cool completely before serving. «««

≫ Dried Cherry Granola *and* Ambrosia Parfaits

These parfaits have a little something for every preference. Like something crunchy and nutty for breakfast? It's there. Like fresh fruit to start off the day? Accounted for. Yogurt typically part of your morning routine? Check. While both the granola and the ambrosia can stand alone, they're an ideal pairing. **SERVES 4 TO 6**

YOU WILL NEED

for the granola

1½ cups rolled oats

½ cup whole almonds, roasted

¼ cup pumpkin seeds, roasted

¼ cup sunflower seeds, roasted

½ cup sweetened coconut

¼ cup honey

¼ cup olive oil

2 tablespoons packed
    light brown sugar

1½ teaspoons ground allspice

1 teaspoon almond extract

½ teaspoon sea salt

¾ cup dried cherries

for the ambrosia

½ fresh pineapple, peeled, cored,
    and cut into chunks

1 orange, peeled and segments
    roughly chopped

1 cup chopped strawberries

½ cup sweetened coconut

1 cup whole yogurt

1 teaspoon almond extract

TO MAKE

1. *Prepare the Granola:* Preheat the oven to 300°F. Oil a large, rimmed baking sheet and set aside.

2. Place all the ingredients except for the dried cherries into a large bowl. Stir with a mixing spoon to coat completely.

3. Spread the mixture evenly onto the prepared baking sheet. Bake for 35 to 40 minutes, stirring every 10 minutes, until evenly browned and fragrant.

4. Remove the baking sheet from the oven. Let the granola cool in the pan for 10 minutes, and then transfer to a large mixing bowl. Stir in the dried cherries. Let cool completely, then transfer to an airtight container. Use within 3 or 4 weeks.

5. *Prepare the Ambrosia:* Combine all the ingredients in a medium mixing bowl. Stir with a mixing spoon until well incorporated.

6. *Assemble the Parfaits:* Place about ¼ to ½ cup granola into the bottom of a lidded glass container, such as a mason or Weck jar. You can use either 4-ounce or 8-ounce jars, depending on the number of picnickers and the size of the portions you'd like to serve. Cover with ¼ to ½ cup ambrosia. Repeat with the remaining granola and ambrosia and additional jars. Cover each jar with a lid and keep chilled until serving time. ≪

»» Egg, Bacon, *and* Veggie Ramekins

While I love a shared dish, there's something about individual portions that I find incredibly com-forting. In this recipe, eggs, bacon, and vegetables are baked in ramekins and topped with sharp, pungent Gorgonzola cheese. A simple yet satisfying dish that garners many compliments whenever I serve it. **SERVES 6**

YOU WILL NEED

Butter, for greasing

6 strips thick-cut bacon

10 ounces Brussels sprouts, quartered, or 1 bunch of asparagus cut into bite-size pieces

10 eggs

1 cup heavy cream

Pinch of sea salt

Dash of hot sauce

2 ounces Gorgonzola cheese, crumbled

Several grinds of black pepper

TO MAKE

1. Heat the oven to 375°F. Butter six 8-ounce ramekins and set aside.

2. Place a wire cooling rack on a rimmed baking sheet. Lay the bacon slices, evenly spaced, over the wire rack and cook for 15 to 30 minutes, until cooked through and a little crispy. Cooking times will vary based on the thickness of the slices.

3. Transfer the bacon onto a plate covered in paper towels and set aside. Remove the wire rack from the baking sheet, leaving the bacon grease in the pan.

4. Toss the quartered Brussels sprouts or asparagus pieces and the bacon grease on the baking sheet. Return the pan to the oven for 20 minutes for Brussels sprouts or 10 minutes for asparagus. Remove the pan from the oven and set aside.

5. In a medium mixing bowl, beat the eggs with the cream, salt, and the hot sauce until thoroughly mixed.

6. Pour the egg mixture into the ramekins, dividing it evenly.

7. Crumble up the bacon. Evenly distribute the bacon and Brussels sprouts or asparagus among the ramekins. Top with the crumbled Gorgonzola and freshly ground black pepper.

8. Bake for 30 to 40 minutes, until the eggs are cooked through. Let cool for 10 minutes before serving.

Note: You can also assemble these the night before, leave them in the fridge overnight, then bake them in the morning before leaving for the picnic. «««

» bird-watching «

PICNIC

When I was a teenager, likely around age fifteen or sixteen, I started designing the type of woman I hoped to one day become. Informed by female characters found in film and literature, as well as iconic artists, writers, and other creative types, I began mentally crafting a checklist of whom I hoped to grow into. On that list, along with a woman who enjoyed listening to chamber music, baked a fine cake, and enjoyed a daily cocktail, I knew I wanted to become a naturalist.

My mother, though possessed of a number of skills, could never be called much of a "natural woman." The same can be said of my father and of most members of my close family. Perhaps in part motivated to know things they didn't, I decided early on to learn plant and animal identification, as well as other types of botanical and biological information. I've been on a quest ever since.

While I can now distinguish an oak from a maple, and yarrow from Queen Anne's lace, I still have a good deal to learn about birds. I'm not an avid birder, but the idea of languidly sitting in a portable chair, warm drink to the left, identification guide to the right, and a pair of binoculars fixed squarely on a tufted titmouse or yellow warbler calls to me in the most profound way. Tuning in to birdsong also appeals to me, especially having recently learned that the calls of birds give a good overview of what is happening in the area.

This picnic celebrates birds and their awe-inspiring contributions to ecosystems. Incorporating foods made by birds as well as those meant to honor them, a picnic with a birding focus is fun, visually arresting, and, at least for me, humbling. Birds can do astounding feats with their bodies, and, in the process, aid the rest of the habitat they reside in. For example, bird calls alert other creatures to predators or threats. Their lofty position and literal "bird's-eye view" give them keen insight into their entire environment. We humans would do well to learn from their example and help others as we help ourselves.

SELECT A SITE

Choose a location known to house a great number of migratory birds. This could be your porch or backyard or a bird sanctuary, botanical garden, or arboretum. Anywhere that's a known thoroughfare or habitat for birds would work wonderfully.

BIRD SKETCHES

Whether you're a third-generation birding enthusiast like my talented friend R. Brooke Priddy Conrad, featured in these photos, or simply a budding naturalist, bring along some paints and pens and a sketchbook, and do your best to render images of the birds you see. Then you'll have a keepsake of the occasion long after the day has passed.

JOURNAL NOTES

Alongside images of the birds, jot down notes relevant to their physical and auditory characteristics. Making note of colors, plumage patterns, calls, and other distinguishing traits will aid you in being able to properly identify specific species in the future.

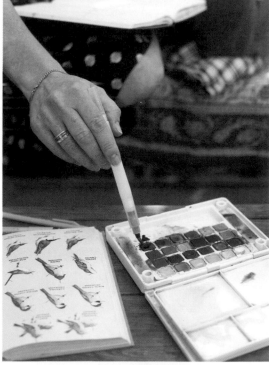

BIRD-WATCHING

There's a reason multitudes of people the world over enjoy watching birds. It's entertaining, educational, and calming, and it's all free. Do consider investing in a decent pair of binoculars, either new or used. Turn your gaze to the trees and behold the splendor of the many winged beauties above.

BIRDING GUIDES

The appearance of different bird species in an area is informed by climate, environment, and topography. A birding guide specific to your given location will prove indispensable in identification. There are also auditory guides available, either to purchase in CD form or to download online. Sometimes it's the uniqueness of a bird's call that is the deciding factor in deciphering who's who.

★ to SAVOR & SIP ★

≫ Pickled Eggs

It wouldn't be proper to have a bird-inspired picnic without an egg-focused dish. Pickled eggs take care of that necessity. Pickling eggs is a wonderful means of using up a fair amount of eggs at once, should you find yourself in possession of a goodly lot of them. The flavor and texture are best within a few days of preparation. **MAKES 1 DOZEN EGGS**

YOU WILL NEED

3 cups water

1 cup apple cider vinegar

1 large beet, quartered

2 garlic cloves, sliced

1 tablespoon honey

1 tablespoon black peppercorns

2 teaspoons sea salt

3 to 4 fresh thyme sprigs

1 dozen hard-boiled eggs, shelled

TO MAKE

1. Combine the all ingredients except for the hard-boiled eggs in a medium saucepan. Bring to a boil, then reduce the heat to low and simmer for 20 minutes.

2. Remove the saucepan from the heat, cover with a lid, and allow to cool completely.

3. Place the eggs in a lidded container (a glass canister is very handy for this purpose). Pour the cooled brine over the eggs. Transfer to the refrigerator.

4. Keep the pickled eggs chilled until serving time. They are best within 2 or 3 days of making. ≪

⟫ Carbonara Nests

This entrée playfully mimics a magpie's nest, full of bright bits and bobs. The pasta is swirled up in individual small pans, creating the "nest" shapes, while "eggs" come in the form of bocconcini (small mozzarella balls), grape tomatoes, and olives. Roasted broccoli rabe stands in for twigs and branches. SERVES 4 TO 5

YOU WILL NEED

1 pound spaghetti (dry)

4 bacon slices

½ pound broccoli rabe

1 garlic clove, finely minced

¾ teaspoon sea salt

Several grinds of black pepper

4 egg yolks

1 cup lightly packed grated Parmesan cheese

½ cup heavy cream

¼ teaspoon freshly grated nutmeg

2 tablespoons olive oil

Cherry or grape tomatoes, to serve

Green olives, to serve

Bocconcini, to serve

Chopped fresh parsley, to serve

TO MAKE

1. Set out 4 or 5 small ovenproof frying pans. Preheat the oven to 350°F. Cook the pasta according to the directions on the package.

2. Meanwhile, cook the bacon in a heavy frying pan over medium heat, until cooked through but not too crispy. Remove the bacon from the pan and drain on paper towels, reserving the bacon grease in the pan.

3. Toss the broccoli rabe with the bacon grease in the frying pan. Sauté until a bit browned, about 10 minutes.

4. Add the garlic, ¼ teaspoon of the salt, and a few grinds of black pepper to the broccoli rabe. Sauté constantly for 1 minute, then remove from the heat.

5. In a medium bowl, whisk together the egg yolks, Parmesan, heavy cream, the remaining ½ teaspoon of salt, the nutmeg, and a few grinds of pepper.

6. Drain the pasta when it is done, then toss it in a large bowl with the olive oil. Add the egg mixture and toss well to coat evenly.

7. Place a baseball- to softball-size scoop of pasta into each small frying pan.

8. Form the pasta in each pan into a nest shape, pushing it up around the sides and indenting the center a bit.

9. Cut the bacon into bite-size pieces. Scatter evenly over the pasta.

10. Top with the broccoli rabe. Bake for 20 minutes. (This step will make the pasta hold its shape.)

11. Before serving, top the "nests" with cherry tomatoes, olives, bocconcini, and a sprinkle of chopped fresh parsley. ⟪

⟫⟫ Birdseed Cookies

Early every December, I host a cookie exchange at my home. Several years ago, my friend Rachel's contribution was what she called Birdseed Cookies. This is my homage both to Rachel's cookies and to the mix of nuts and seeds in birdseed blends. Though it may be "for the birds," it's amazingly tasty for the human set, too. MAKES 2 DOZEN COOKIES

YOU WILL NEED

¾ cup rolled oats

½ cup millet

1½ cups all-purpose flour

½ teaspoon baking soda

½ teaspoon baking powder

½ teaspoon sea salt

½ teaspoon ground nutmeg

1 cup packed light brown sugar

¾ cup (1½ sticks) unsalted butter, at room temperature

2 teaspoons vanilla extract

2 eggs

1 cup roasted and salted peanuts

½ cup raisins

⅓ cup roasted and salted sunflower seeds

TO MAKE

1. Preheat the oven to 300°F. Spread the rolled oats and millet over a rimmed baking sheet. Toast in the oven for 10 to 15 minutes, until fragrant and slightly browned. Set aside to cool. Turn off the oven.

2. In a medium bowl, sift together the flour, baking soda, baking powder, salt, and nutmeg. Set aside.

3. In a large bowl, using an electric mixer on medium speed, beat together the brown sugar, butter, vanilla, and eggs until pale and creamy, around 3 to 4 minutes.

4. With the mixer on low, beat in the flour mixture just until fully combined. Stir in the toasted oats and millet and the peanuts, raisins, and sunflower seeds. Transfer the dough to a lidded container. Refrigerate for 1 hour.

5. Heat the oven to 350°F. Line two rimmed baking sheets with silicone mats or parchment paper. Spoon 1 tablespoon of batter for each cookie onto the baking sheets, spacing cookies 1 inch apart.

6. Bake for 20 minutes, or until lightly browned, rotating the baking sheets halfway through the baking time. Let the cookies cool for 10 minutes on the baking sheets, then transfer to cooling racks to cool completely. ⟪⟪

» table to farm «

PICNIC

Every summer my husband, son, and I pack a picnic and make our way to various area farms. Sponsored by a local nonprofit, ASAP (Appalachian Sustainable Agriculture Project), the Family Farm Tour that we participate in annually covers several counties spread across the mountains of western North Carolina. Over the course of one weekend, we traverse the region. Our stops include a wide array of enterprises, from creameries to hot pepper farms to those raising a variety of livestock.

When my son was eight months old, we packed a picnic, gathered up a friend to join us, and headed to Hickory Nut Gap, a multigenerational farm in nearby Fairview, North Carolina. My husband and I had visited the farm many times before because it sells apples and apple products each autumn and is simply a beautiful place to visit. On the weekend of the Family Farm Tour, Hickory Nut Gap was our first stop. As I signed in and handed over the fee, I quickly glanced at the other names on the sign-up sheet.

Written directly above my name was "Jenifer Altman." Jen and I had been in contact online for over a year, but we had never met in person. I quickly looked up from the registration table, glanced around, spotted a red-haired woman, and yelled, "Jen! It's Ashley!" That fateful encounter established a friendship and many professional collaborations.

I've since visited Hickory Nut Gap many times, every time with a picnic lunch in tow. Now that I'm a parent, it's become an even more magical place, rife with creeks, barns, chicks, horses, corn mazes, and countless places for Huxley to enjoy and explore. My idea with this Table to Farm Picnic is to turn the "Farm to Table" model on its head, returning full circle to literally take the table to the farm, bringing along not only a local-foods picnic but a DIY portable table for picnicking on.

For this picnic, we chose Hickory Nut Gap's neighbor, Flying Cloud Farm. Not only are the farms adjacent to each other, but they're run by cousins! Annie Perkinson and her two daughters, along with her niece, joined us for the feast, while her husband, Isaiah, worked the fields on his tractor. A true "Table to Farm" experience if there ever was one! Enjoy the farms in your area and all the flavors and fun they have to offer, bringing them from the produce-laden table at the tailgate market right on back to a handmade table out there in the fields.

✴ to MAKE & DO

SELECT A SITE

I encourage you to have this picnic on an actual farm. Many farms are regularly open to the public, whether on weekends, on select days, or annually for special Farm Tours. Even better, earlier in the week, purchase the produce you intend to use for your picnic from the farm you've chosen to visit. You'll then be able to experience the full sensory potential of a working farm, from its flavors to its sights, smells, and sounds.

TRANSPORTABLE TABLE

Many of us are familiar with the concept of "farm to table" eating. Here I'm flipping the phrase, encouraging you to bring a table to the farm! This table is supereasy to craft, and can be enjoyed at many other picnics as well as this one. To make it happen, all you need is a simple wooden crate and a wooden surface.

✴ diy portable table

If you think picnicking is limited to blankets on the ground or freestanding picnic tables with built-in benches, think again. With a few tools and supplies, you can create your own portable picnic table. Place it atop a picnic blanket, gather 'round, and you've got the best of all possible picnic arrangements!

YOU WILL NEED

Wooden crate (see Note)

Wooden boards, for tabletop (see Note)

1 × 2-inch wooden boards, for "lip" (see Note)

Wood screws, for attaching the lip to the tabletop

Metal outdoor gate handle (optional)

½-inch screws, for attaching the handle (optional)

Paint or wood stain (optional)

TO MAKE

1. For the base, you'll need a wooden crate or similarly sized wooden box. These can be found either in vintage form, at antiques stores and online, or new at many craft and home goods stores. The base can also serve as a container to carry picnic supplies to the site, which is particularly handy.

2. For the top, choose one large piece of wood or several boards that can be connected. Make the tabletop four or so inches wider than the wooden box on all sides. Cut four lengths of 1 × 2-inch board that are ⅛ inch longer than the four sides of the box; these will create a rectangle with an inside edge that is slightly larger than the outside dimensions of the box. Screw the lengths of 1 × 2-inch to the bottom side of the tabletop in a rectangle shape, being careful that the screws don't poke through the top side (the ends should meet but *not* overlap). This rectangle will serve as a "lip," helping to keep the tabletop from sliding once placed on the box. If desired, screw an outdoor gate handle onto the underside of the tabletop. This will make it easy to carry to the picnic site in one hand.

3. If you like, you can paint or stain the tabletop and the crate to match or to complement each other. If you want a rustic look, sand some of the edges to distress the finish a bit.

Note: Wooden crates vary by size but are generally around 1 foot wide and 1½ feet long. For the tabletop you will need enough wood to extend 4 or so inches on each side beyond the length and width of whatever crate that you choose. For example, if you use a crate that is 12 inches wide by 18 inches long, you will need a board, or boards, that add up to about 26 inches long and about 20 inches wide. For the "lip" that holds the boards together and helps keep the tabletop in place, you will need lengths of 1 × 2-inch board that are long enough to go around the circumference of the crate. A standard 6-foot length would be perfect to provide all the cuts you will need.

FARM BOUQUETS

A number of farms grow flowers alongside their corn, tomatoes, and zucchini. Some offer bouquets already assembled on-site while others allow you to pick your own for a small fee. Whether premade or handcrafted by you, a farm-fresh bouquet adds a wonderful pop of color to your picnic table.

PATTERNS IN NATURE

The Fibonacci sequence, or series, is named after Leonardo of Pisa, an Italian mathematician also known as Fibonacci. The Fibonacci sequence is recursive, meaning it builds on itself, and it is generated by adding the two previous numbers in the series: 0, 1, 1, 2, 3, 5, 8, 13, 21, 34, 55, 89, 144, 233, 377, 610, 987 . . . The mathematics of the "golden ratio" and of the Fibonacci series are intimately interconnected.

Maybe the most remarkable feature of the series is the manner in which it evidences itself repeatedly in nature. It is made manifest in the patterns in which a nautilus shell curls, a hurricane advances, a wave forms, a fern frond unfurls, a sunflower head and aloe plant spiral, a pineapple sprouts fruit, an artichoke flowers, a pinecone is arranged, and even a human fingerprint is configured.

During this picnic, I invite you to look for patterns in nature. If sunflowers are available on the farm, they'll be a fine indicator of the "silent series" at work. In a world that often seems random and disparate, I find it remarkably reassuring to witness such order quietly on display.

to SAVOR & SIP

⟫⟫ Zucchini Gratin

There can never be too many ways to prepare zucchini. This option, which enrobes the prolific summer squash in a robust cheese sauce, might quickly become your favorite means of serving it. Choose whatever cheese you most prefer or a blend of several. **SERVES 8 TO 10**

YOU WILL NEED

4 tablespoons (½ stick) salted butter, at room temperature

¼ cup all-purpose flour

2 cups buttermilk, at room temperature

1 cup heavy cream, at room temperature

1 cup grated cheese (Gruyère, Gouda, Comte, and/or cheddar)

½ cup grated Parmesan cheese (for the sauce)

½ teaspoon ground chipotle or cayenne

⅛ teaspoon freshly grated nutmeg

1 teaspoon sea salt

Several grinds of black pepper

2 pounds zucchini, cut into ⅛-inch slices

for the bread crumb topping

Enough toasted bread to make 2 cups of bread crumbs from approximately 4–6 slices of bread, depending on size

4 tablespoons (½ stick) salted butter

¼ cup grated Parmesan cheese

TO MAKE

1. Preheat the oven to 375°F. Butter a 9 × 9-inch baking pan or a gratin pan of similar capacity.

2. In a small bowl, using a spoon or spatula, work the softened butter into the flour until fully incorporated. Transfer to a medium saucepan. Cook over low heat until the mixture becomes saucy.

3. Whisk the buttermilk and cream together in a small bowl. Stir into the butter and flour mixture, a little bit at a time. When it is an even consistency, stir in the grated cheese and Parmesan. Add the chipotle, nutmeg, salt, and pepper and stir until all the ingredients are fully incorporated. Remove from the heat.

4. Layer half of the zucchini slices in the bottom of the prepared gratin pan and then drizzle half of the cheese sauce over them. Layer the rest of the zucchini over that and then pour the rest of the cheese sauce evenly over the top.

5. *Make the Bread Crumbs:* Toast enough bread to make 2 cups of bread crumbs, and pulse in a food processor to crumble. Measure out 2 cups into a small bowl. Melt the butter and continue to heat until it starts to brown, then pour it over the bread crumbs. Add the Parmesan and stir until fully combined. Scatter the prepared crumbs evenly over the last layer of cheese sauce.

6. Bake for about 45 minutes, until the bread crumbs are golden. Allow to sit for 15 to 20 minutes before serving. ⟪⟪

⟫ Gazpacho

I could very easily eat gazpacho every day, all summer long (and I sometimes do!). When toma-toes, peppers, and summer squashes are ripe, the flavor of this cold soup is incomparable. What distinguishes my version from others is a quick sweating, or cooking down, of the vegetables before pureeing. The inclusion of that little bit of heat caramelizes and sweetens up the vegetables, creating a soup that is profoundly satisfying on a warm day. **SERVES 8 TO 10**

YOU WILL NEED

3 garlic cloves

Pinch of coarse salt

½ cup olive oil

1 large onion, diced

3 medium carrots, peeled
   and diced

2 red, yellow, or orange
   bell peppers, diced

1 pound yellow squash
   or zucchini, diced

1 quart organic vegetable juice

3 tablespoons white wine, red wine,
   or balsamic vinegar

Juice of 1 lime

1 tablespoon Worcestershire sauce

A few dashes of hot sauce

1 teaspoon ground cumin

2 teaspoons sea salt

Several grinds of black pepper

3 pounds fresh tomatoes, diced

2 pounds cucumbers, seeded
   and diced

optional toppings

Almond slivers

Toast points

Chopped fresh parsley, cilantro,
   or lemon balm

Hot sauce

TO MAKE

1. Mince the garlic finely and then chop a pinch of coarse salt into it. Leave to sit for a few minutes while you prepare the vegetables.

2. Warm the olive oil in a stockpot over medium-high heat. Add the onion, carrots, bell peppers, squash, and prepared garlic and reduce the heat to low. Cook for 10 to 12 minutes, until the onion is translucent and the vegetables are fragrant and limp.

3. Add the vegetable juice, wine, lime juice, Worcestershire sauce, hot sauce, cumin, sea salt, and black pepper to the pot. Cook for 2 more minutes.

4. Remove from the heat, and set aside for 20 to 30 minutes, until the soup mixture is not hot anymore (warm is OK).

5. Working in batches, pour the cooled mixture into a food processor and pulse until there are no big pieces but it is still a bit textured. Transfer to a large bowl.

6. Working in batches, pulse the diced tomatoes in the food processor until a similar consistency is achieved, then stir them into the vegetable mixture in the bowl. Stir in the diced cucumbers.

7. Cover the bowl and place in the refrigerator to chill. Gazpacho can be made the night before serving; in fact, doing so helps the flavors to "set up" and develop. To serve, ladle the soup into bowls. Garnish with optional toppings as desired. ⟪

»» Chimichurri Chicken

Of Argentinian origin, chimichurri is a green, herb-based sauce meant to accompany grilled or roasted meats. It is immensely flavorful without being overwhelming. Here I've tossed the sauce with roast chicken. You might have a little extra chimichurri left over, depending on the size of your chicken and how liberally you dress it. Store any unused portion in the refrigerator and consider having it with other meats (grilled steak is especially delicious) or eggs. **SERVES 4 TO 6, DEPENDING ON THE SIZE OF YOUR CHICKEN**

YOU WILL NEED

2 garlic cloves

½ teaspoon coarse sea salt

Bunch of fresh cilantro

Bunch of fresh parsley, stems chopped off

Leaves from about 4 sprigs of fresh oregano

½ cup olive oil

¼ cup sherry vinegar, red wine vinegar, or white wine vinegar

Juice of ½ lime

A few dashes hot sauce

½ teaspoon fine sea salt

Several grinds of black pepper

Meat from 1 whole roast chicken (set the bones aside for making stock)

TO MAKE

1. Mince the garlic very finely, and then chop the coarse salt into it. Leave to sit and mellow for 20 minutes.

2. Pulse the minced garlic and all the ingredients except the chicken in a food processor or blender until saucy.

3. In a large bowl, toss the sauce with the pulled chicken, cover, and refrigerate for at least 1 hour before serving. «««

»» Peach *and* Lemon Verbena Clafoutis

Pronounced kla-foo-TEA, this French, custard-like dish is quite possibly the easiest dessert I have ever made. Typically baked with cherries, my version uses fresh, ripe peaches and fragrant lemon verbena for a sweet, bright flavor and fragrance. A good amount of eggs are used, so the clafoutis will behave very much like a soufflé when it first emerges from the oven, puffing up high and slowly deflating over several minutes (the flavor is undiminished, though). **SERVES 6 TO 8**

YOU WILL NEED

3 large ripe peaches

2 tablespoons chopped fresh
   lemon verbena

4 eggs

1 cup heavy cream

¾ cup all-purpose flour

⅔ cup sugar

2 tablespoons brandy

1 tablespoon vanilla extract

¼ teaspoon sea salt

TO MAKE

1. Preheat the oven to 375°F. Butter a 2-quart dish or pie pan and set aside.

2. Cut each peach into quarters, then cut each quarter into ½-inch slices. Fan out the sliced peaches in the bottom of your prepared pan. Scatter the minced lemon verbena over the peaches. Set aside.

3. In a food processor or blender, combine the eggs, cream, flour, sugar, brandy, vanilla, and salt. Process about 2 to 3 minutes, until all the ingredients are fully combined.

4. Pour the batter over the fruit and lemon verbena. Bake for 45 minutes to 1 hour, until the top is golden and the batter doesn't wobble or jiggle in the center.

5. Allow to cool for at least 30 minutes before serving. ‹‹‹

»» into the woods ««

The woods have always been home to me. There was the first time I saw the Ewok village in the film *Return of the Jedi* when I was seven years old, when I told my young self, silently, that I would love to live somewhere similar. There's the street I lived on from ages eight to twelve in Chesapeake, Virginia—*Forest Road*—and the woods I played in there. There's the converted tobacco barn in the deeply wooded town of Montreat, North Carolina, that my mother, brother, and I called home for a far-too-brief seven months.

Later, in my early twenties, a former boyfriend and I shared a home in Weaverville, North Carolina, lovingly crafted by his father over the course of ten years, composed entirely of a wooden interior gleaned from trees on their forested acreage. Now, there's the wooded cove I call home in Candler, North Carolina, adjacent to a 300-plus acres of heavily forested nature preserve. Finally, there's my son, Huxley, whose name translates to both "woodsman" and "a clearing in a forest." The woods and I, we're tethered to each other, it would seem.

I think what speaks to me the most about wooded environments are their natural, inherent tendencies toward change. Emergence, growth, decay, and renewal are what enable them to thrive, to adapt, to endure. There is no stasis in the woods. They are always in flux, no matter how slowly. I often feel the same way—unfixed, fluid, adapting to whatever the day or occasion brings—so that I too might persevere and grow.

A picnic sited in the woods is a wonderful opportunity to celebrate change. There are the Walt Whitman lines in "Song of Myself" that I have long loved: "Do I contradict myself? / Very well then I contradict myself, / (I am large, I contain multitudes.)" The forest changes, as do we. We learn to bend in the wind like the tree, or to break instead. Not only is a wooded setting simply a lovely location to enjoy a meal, it's a living "school" of sorts, with so many lessons about life on offer.

✳ *to* MAKE & DO

SELECT A SITE

This picnic is all about forests and wooded areas. Choose your picnicking site with that at the forefront of your mind. Private land owned by you or your friends or family, state or national parks, forested areas on college campuses—any of these areas would be ideal candidates for an Into the Woods Picnic.

MAKE ROCK STACKS

The picnic area shown in these photographs is home to a large number of rock stacks, also known as *cairns*. I don't know who originally created them, but they have been there for years. The mystery surrounding their creation gives them an added allure, allowing one to wonder, if you're at all like me, whether it was even human hands that stacked them in the first place. If your wooded area is home to a creek or otherwise populated by rocks, consider creating a rock stack of your own. If it stands the test of time and weather, it will be an unexpected yet welcome sight to anyone who encounters it.

BUILD FAIRY HOUSES

There is a folk myth that persists globally about the existence of fairies. Tiny beings responsible for helping nature hum along on schedule, fairies are believed to be a bit shy, and often just out of human viewing. While picnicking, consider building homes for these diminutive, beneficial creatures. Sticks, stones, moss, flowers, leaves, or any other bits of natural ephemera all work equally well for festooning and decorating.

✳ *to* BEHOLD & EXPLORE

EMERGING GROWTH

Early spring would be a lovely time to have a wooded picnic. The poison ivy, bugs, and humidity are still a ways off, the mornings are cool, and the sun isn't terribly punishing just yet. On your way to your picnicking site, and once you arrive, take note of what's emerging. On branches, out of the soil, on creek banks—and all around really—will be buds, flowers, mushrooms, and many other signs of spring's emerging from her wintertime slumber.

BEAUTY IN DECAY

It's inevitable that, at some point during your time in the forest, you'll find a fallen tree, if not many. Wind, snow, lightning, disease, insects, and beavers can all bring down a tree. While it might at first seem like a loss for such a wooded heavyweight to have fallen, dead trees are actually teeming with life. Decomposers like bacteria, fungi, and worms move in, gaining nourishment from the tree, while other creatures such as foxes use it as shelter. During your picnic, take a moment to appreciate the beauty and bounty manifest in decay. The wheel of life is round, with today's life feeding tomorrow's.

✳ to SAVOR & SIP ✳

››› Watercress *and* Feta Salad

Watercress is a leafy green typically found growing beside creek beds. As such, including it in this picnic is a gentle nod to the many edibles typically found in forested areas. It has a bit of a peppery bite to it, which is balanced perfectly by the feta. **SERVES 4 TO 6**

YOU WILL NEED

for the vinaigrette

⅔ cup olive oil

¼ cup white wine vinegar

1 tablespoon honey

¼ teaspoon sea salt

A few grinds of black pepper

for the salad

2 bunches of watercress

1 cup diced pickled beets, cut into small chunks

1 cup crumbled feta

TO MAKE

1. *Prepare the Dressing:* Place all the vinaigrette ingredients in a lidded container, such as a mason jar. Shake vigorously to fully combine.

2. *Prepare the Salad:* Roughly tear the watercress into 1- to 2-inch pieces. Place in a medium bowl.

3. Add the pickled beets and the feta to the bowl. Pour in about ½ cup of the vinaigrette, reserving the extra for later use. Using salad tongs, toss everything together until completely combined and coated with the vinaigrette.

4. Plate individual portions and serve immediately. ‹‹‹

⟫⟫ Mushroom Beef Stew

Mushrooms are another edible food often viewed in wooded areas. I call for crimini or oyster mush-rooms here for a more robust flavor, but if those can't be sourced, button mushrooms will work, too. Rendered into a hearty beef stew, they make exactly the kind of fare you want filling your belly when the day calls for forest frolicking! SERVES 6 TO 8

YOU WILL NEED

2 pounds grass-fed beef stew meat

¼ cup high-heat oil of your choice, such as peanut or olive

1 medium onion, diced

3 carrots, cut in ⅛-inch slices

3 stalks of celery, cut into small pieces

3 garlic cloves, minced

2 pounds mixed mushrooms, such as crimini and oyster, sliced

1 quart beef stock

2 cups red wine

1 teaspoon dried thyme

1 teaspoon sea salt

A few grinds of black pepper

¼ cup chopped fresh parsley

TO MAKE

1. In a stockpot over medium-high heat, brown the meat in 2 tablespoons of the oil for about 8 minutes. Transfer the meat and any pan juices into a bowl and set aside.

2. Add 2 more tablespoons of oil to the stockpot over medium-high heat. Add the onion, carrots, and celery and sauté for about 15 minutes, until they are fragrant and browned at the edges.

3. Add the garlic and cook for 1 minute. Add the mushrooms and cook for about 10 more minutes, until their liquid has cooked off.

4. Add the browned meat and pan juices, stock, wine, thyme, and salt and pepper.

5. Reduce the heat to low and simmer for about 2 hours, stirring occasionally, until the liquid has evaporated. Be extra careful for the second half of cooking, making sure it does not scorch at the bottom of the pan. If the liquid evaporates too early, you can add extra stock.

6. Season with additional salt if needed. Stir in the parsley, and then remove from the heat.

7. Allow the stew to cool for 15 to 20 minutes then serve, or store in a lidded container in the refrigerator and reheat before serving. ⟪⟪

»» Maple Poundcake

Maples are deciduous trees offering lovely foliage and delightful syrup, among many other things. During autumn walks, I love encountering a vibrant red- or yellow-leafed maple in the forest. Their jewel tones are simply breathtaking. Here I'm offering a maple-laced poundcake. It's moist yet sturdy—just the kind of cake required to withstand the rigors of walking through the woods to secure the perfect forested picnic spot. MAKES ONE 9 × 5-INCH LOAF

YOU WILL NEED

4 eggs, yolks and whites separated

1 cup (2 sticks) unsalted butter, at room temperature

1 cup sugar

½ cup maple syrup

1 teaspoon vanilla extract

2 cups all-purpose flour

½ teaspoon sea salt

Fresh berries, to serve

TO MAKE

1. Preheat the oven to 350°F. Lightly butter a 9 × 5-inch loaf pan and set aside.

2. Using an electric mixer or whisk, beat the egg whites in a medium bowl until light and billowy. Set aside.

3. In a large bowl, using an electric mixer, cream the butter, sugar, and maple syrup until light and fluffy, about 3 to 4 minutes. Beat in the vanilla extract.

4. Add the egg yolks, one at a time, beating well and scraping the bowl and beaters with a spatula after each addition. Using a spatula, gently fold in the beaten egg whites until fully incorporated.

5. Whisk together the flour and salt in a medium bowl. Add the flour mixture to the egg mixture, 1 cup at a time, scraping down the bowl and beaters after each addition.

6. Pour the batter into the prepared pan and use a spatula to spread it evenly.

7. Bake for 1 hour and 20 to 25 minutes, until the top is golden brown and a knife inserted into the center comes out clean.

8. Allow the cake to cool in the pan for 15 minutes, then remove it from the pan and leave to cool on a wire rack for an additional 15 minutes.

9. To serve, slice into 1-inch-thick slices and scatter with berries. «‹

» children's «

PICNIC

From ages two to eight, I lived in the bustling surfside city of Virginia Beach, Virginia. When my brother and I weren't in preschool or school, chances are we were swimming in a community pool, at the beach, or somewhere else romping around outside. The mother of two young children on a modest budget, my mom took full advantage of all of the outdoor, mostly free activities available in our area.

High on her list of places to go when the sun was shining and our energy levels were in an ever-upward arc were playgrounds. I have an incredibly distinct memory of being pushed higher and higher on a swing as Mom ran beneath it performing her signature "underdog" maneuver. I can still recall the creak of the swing set and its "whoosh!" as Mom pushed me ever skyward. Though we likely only stayed on the swing for ten or fifteen minutes, in my mind's eye we were there for hours. I remember colossal playground structures we'd gleefully climb on, and the skinned knees we'd happily acquire in the process.

Inevitably, after our playground forays, there would be a simple picnic. Drinks and snacks were doled out, and the three of us would recline and relax and regroup from our frolicking, often in the company of a handful of our friends and their parents. They were simple but so very satisfying, those playground picnics. She may have been short on cash, but Mom was rich with an ability to craft lasting memories from humble resources.

If you have children, inevitably at some point in time you will have a picnic with them. For this occasion, though, I encourage you to make the picnic completely and wholly *about* them. From the location to the food to the activities, a picnic focusing entirely on children (whether your own, your relatives', or those in your community) will present lasting memories for everyone who attends. Our picnics were simple yet special, and they will always been treasured. I wish the same for you.

✳ to MAKE & DO

SELECT A SITE

Hosting this picnic at a playground is highly recommended. Children will get to run and play and exercise while the parents can chat and enjoy one another's company. Everyone wins! If it's a hot, sunny day, bring along some natural bug spray and sunscreen for those children (and adults!) who might need it.

KIDS CORNHOLE

Essentially a game of tossing small beanbags into a hole cut into wooden board, cornhole is decidedly addictive. Children and adults alike love it. Historically, it is played with two boards and eight bags, with competing teams of two. In this version for small children, simply allow each player to toss all the bags (or four of one color) before moving to the next player.

Scoring is super simple: A bag in the hole is 3 points; a bag on the board is 1 point; a bag hanging from the board but not touching the ground is 1 point; a bag hanging but touching the ground is 0 points, and any bags on the ground are 0 points. Have a player toss all the bags, take score, and then move on to the next player. The highest score wins!

✳ to BEHOLD & EXPLORE

I SPY

My parents split up when I was one and a half years old. For several years, my weekends were alternated between Mom and Dad. Sometimes Dad would come to us, in Virginia Beach, and sometimes we'd go visit him, up in Washington, D.C. On those trips north, car games were indispensible for keeping us occupied (this was long before the days of electronic in-car devices!) and for helping Dad remain sane with two young children in the car for four hours. *I Spy with My Little Eye* was one game we turned to again and again, and it would be so much fun to play at a children's picnic.

You'll need at least two players. Have one of the players choose something visible to everyone gathered (any item will work: a dog, a park bench, a swing, a pine tree, a stroller, etc.). The player will then say, "I spy with my little eye, something that _____." They'll provide some kind of identifying feature of the item in question, such as its color, or shape, or scent, or texture, or even what letter it begins with ("begins with D" if it's a dog). The other player(s) will each ask a question, in turn, to aid in identifying the object. The player who is running the game can answer only with "yes" or "no." Players continue asking until the object is correctly guessed.

✳ diy cornhole board

Not only is cornhole plain old fun, it also helps children learn dexterity and coordination. When not in use, store the board away from the elements, such as in a basement or garage.

YOU WILL NEED

1½-inch wood screws

Two 1 × 6-inch wooden boards, 4 feet long

Two 1 × 6-inch boards, 22 inches long

One 2 × 4-foot panel or piece of plywood

Paint

Outdoor metal handle (optional)

¾-inch screws for handle

Two 2 × 2-inch boards, 3 feet long

One 2 × 2-inch board, cut to ¼ inch longer than the length of the crate

Standard wooden crate (approximately 1 foot × 1½ feet × 9 inches high)

Eight small beanbags, for tossing

TO MAKE

1. With an electric screwdriver and 1½-inch wood screws, screw the *narrow edges* of the four 1 × 6-inch boards to the back of the panel along its outer perimeter so that the flat sides are flush with the panel's edge; you will be inserting the screws through the top of the panel.

2. At the corners, screw the boards to one another.

3. Trace a 6-inch circle onto the panel, centered 6 inches from one of the short sides. Drill a large hole inside of the traced circle. Using the hole as a starting point, cut out the circle along the traced outline with a jigsaw.

4. Paint the board however you like. Attach the metal handle to the side with the ¾-inch screws if you like (making it easier to carry to picnics!).

5. Screw the 3-foot-long 2 × 2-inch boards to the ends of the long 2 × 2-inch board, making a "U" shape.

6. Lay the U-shaped board on the ground with the 3-inch ends facing up.

7. Place the back edge of the wooden crate on top of the U-shaped board.

8. Place the panel over the crate, so that the inside of the crate is lined up with the hole, and the game is on an angle. Toss beanbags into the hole.

✳ to SAVOR & SIP ✳

≫ Grilled PB&J

I have yet to meet any child who doesn't like peanut butter and jelly sandwiches. Even those with food sensitivities can get in on the action, via almond or other nut or seed butters. This recipe was inspired by my friend Nate Kelly and the grilled PB&Nutella offered by his Asheville-based food truck, "The Low Down." Nate's truck is often docked in a parking lot facing a building my young son sometimes takes gymnastics lessons in. Right after class, he slips on his shoes, grabs my hand, and sweetly requests to cross the street for one of Nate's warm, oozing, delicious, decadent sandwiches. Use whatever jam, jelly, or fruit preserves you have on hand. **SERVINGS VARY**

YOU WILL NEED

Bread slices, 2 per child

Melted butter, 2 teaspoons per child

Peanut butter, 2 tablespoons per child

Jelly or jam, 1 tablespoon per child

TO MAKE

1. Cut the bread slices into rounds using a circle-shaped cookie cutter. Other large cookie cutters will work as well.

2. Preheat a panini press or griddle.

3. Pour the melted butter onto a plate (you'll need 1 teaspoon for each slice of bread, so 2 teaspoons for 1 sandwich). Dip one side of a slice of bread into the melted butter, then transfer it, buttered side down, to a cutting board.

4. For each sandwich, spread 2 tablespoons of peanut butter on 1 slice of bread. Top with 1 tablespoon of jelly.

5. Butter another slice of bread and place it, buttered side up, on top of the slice with the peanut butter and jelly. Lift the sandwich up using a spatula and transfer it to the panini press or griddle.

6. Cook over medium heat until nicely browned on both sides. ≪

»» Cheesy Kale Chips

Kale chips are popular for a reason. Done right, they're simply delicious. At the photo shoot for this picnic, all eight of the children present ate them by the handful, without any requests (or bribing!) from their parents. Although you can make them ahead of time, they do lose their crunch if there's a good deal of moisture in the atmosphere (like on a humid summer day). MAKES 4 TO 5 CUPS

YOU WILL NEED

2 bunches of kale, de-stemmed, torn into large pieces, washed, and dried

¼ cup olive oil

1 teaspoon sea salt

Freshly cracked black pepper

½ cup lightly packed grated Parmesan cheese

TO MAKE

1. Preheat the oven to 300°F. Spread the kale evenly over two large, rimmed baking sheets.

2. Drizzle each pan of kale with 2 tablespoons of the olive oil. Sprinkle ½ teaspoon of the salt and grind black pepper over each pan of the kale. Using clean hands, toss the kale until the greens are fully coated with oil, salt, and pepper. Spread the kale evenly over the pan.

3. Place one baking sheet onto the upper oven rack and one on a lower rack. Bake for 15 minutes. Switch the baking sheets to opposite oven racks and continue baking for 10 more minutes, checking frequently, until the greens are dark and crispy.

4. Remove the baking sheets from the oven. Distribute the Parmesan evenly over each pan of kale. Return to the oven and bake for 2 to 3 minutes, just until the cheese begins to melt. Remove the pans from the oven and allow the kale to cool completely in the pans.

5. Place the cooled chips into a lidded container. Otherwise, they will quickly become moist and chewy and lose their crunch. These chips are best on the day they are made, and will begin to lose their crunch within several hours of being left out. «««

≫ Fruit Shape Stacks

It seems to me that every child has a latent fruitarian lurking within them. Perhaps it's the inherent sweetness, or the fun colors, or just the abundant juice going every which way when it is chomped on that accounts for the popularity of fruit with the wee set. These stacks are made of a variety of melons cut into different shapes. Colors, flavors, and shapes can all be explored when nibbling these refreshing treats. Educational and delicious = total win. SERVINGS VARY

YOU WILL NEED

Watermelon, cut into triangles

Honeydew, cut into squares

Cantaloupe, cut into spheres

Wooden toothpicks

TO MAKE

1. Place a watermelon triangle on a cutting board. Place a honeydew square on top of the watermelon, and top with a cantaloupe sphere. Thread a wooden toothpick through the fruit to secure. ≪

››› Mango Lassi Ice Pops

Mango lassis are instantly placating. Whether you are five years old or eighty-five, a cool, sweet, creamy beverage on a warm day is a thing of beauty. I used an affordable ice-pop mold purchased online to make these, but you could just as easily use small yogurt containers, plastic juice cups, or other upcycled vessels as molds. **MAKES TWELVE 3-OUNCE POPS**

YOU WILL NEED

2 cups whole milk yogurt

1½ cups ripe mango chunks

½ cup water

2 tablespoons honey

¾ teaspoon ground cardamom

¼ teaspoon ground ginger

TO MAKE

1. Place all the ingredients in a blender. Puree until fully blended.

2. Pour equal amounts into ice-pop molds. Place in the freezer until frozen, at least several hours.

3. At serving, turn the ice-pop mold over, and briefly run under hot water. Tug on the sticks until the pops release from the mold.

4. To serve at the picnic site, either loosen the ice pops with hot water in advance at home, leaving them gently resting in the mold, before putting them into a cooler filled with dry ice, or bring along a thermos of hot water and pour it over the molds at serving time. ‹‹‹

»»» waterside «««

PICNIC

For a good portion of my life, I have lived within close proximity to water. From the salty sands of Virginia Beach to the bullfrog- and turtle-packed shores of the pond beside my grandmother's Chesapeake, Virginia, home, from the emerald-hued waters of Destin, Florida, to the rivers, lakes, and creeks punctuating the landscape of western North Carolina—my current stomping grounds—the trajectory of my life has kept watery settings never far from reach.

My husband's parents live on Siesta Key in Sarasota, Florida. There is a wide stretch of the softest, whitest sand I have ever had the pleasure of experiencing right outside their back door, as their home is located directly on the Gulf of Mexico. They also have a pool. When we visit, our nieces and nephews who live just down the road come over, and there is so much watery mayhem and fun taking place that it's impossible to simply stand by and witness—you have to join in.

Every summer for as long as I can remember, my father's family has convened in Avalon, New Jersey, for one week in July. His seven siblings and their spouses, along with their grown children and their children's spouses and scores of grandchildren, rent several houses and then barely stay in them. From nearly sunrise to often past sunset, they take over a large expanse of beach to read, nap, swim, build sand castles, eat, laugh, play washers, and otherwise enjoy life near the water. When I was younger, I regularly attended these seaside gatherings. Although I haven't gone for some time, I recall with profound clarity the abiding joy those days offered.

Clearly water means a great deal to me. I know it means so very much to others, too. At this picnic, a watery location of your choice holds the promise for good times to come. Take it from me, someone well seasoned in watery ways: picnicking waterside when the mercury peaks and the days are long with heat and humidity will prove relaxing, rejuvenating, and restorative to you and your guests, guaranteed!

✷ to MAKE & DO

SELECT A SITE

This picnic was photographed at Lake Powhatan, a beautiful lake with a wide, sandy beach in Asheville, North Carolina. Besides a lake, any other large body of water near you would work equally well, from salty seas to idyllic ponds. The recipes included here all speak to the need for refreshing foods in such settings, especially when aquatic play is involved. Wherever you choose, don't be surprised if the lovely setting and watery depths induce an awe-inspired reaction in you, too!

BUILD SAND CASTLES

Wherever there is sand, there should be sand castles! A pail packed with sand toys will keep little and big hands busy. Even if children aren't present, there's no shortage of amazing creations that can be rendered out of sand with a bit of imagination.

PLAY FRISBEE

Whenever I think of beach and lakeside activities, I immediately think of playing Frisbee. The sand is soft for running to catch a toss coming your way and also provides a gentle cushion, in the event that you don't quite make it. It's also a great cardiovascular activity, so that even while you're enjoying the ease and comfort of a picnic, you're still getting a bit of exercise while doing so.

✷ to BEHOLD & EXPLORE

GO BEACHCOMBING OR NETCASTING

Scouring the sand, surf, and shoreline for treasures is an all-time favorite activity. One never knows what the tide or current may carry in. Consider bringing a net for gathering up ephemera in the water. Craft a collection from your visits and keep them on display at home, to serve as a living testament to many glorious days spent by the water.

to savor & sip

»» Seafood Sliders

Few flavors rival the taste of fresh seafood. Redolent of salt and sea, shrimp and crab satisfy as few things can when picnicking beach or lakeside. Here I've married ceviche-inspired flavors with the ease and portability of sliders. Lime juice, fresh cilantro, a bit of olive oil, and fresh vegetables let the seafood's flavors remain at the forefront without drowning in a creamy base. A little smear of mayonnaise on the slider bun is suggested but not required. **MAKES 2 DOZEN**

YOU WILL NEED

1 pound peeled and deveined shrimp

3 tablespoons olive oil

1 pound crabmeat

1 red bell pepper, diced

1 small cucumber, peeled, seeded, and diced

2 dozen small cherry tomatoes, sliced

1 large stalk of celery, diced

½ cup bread and butter pickles, diced

Juice from 2¼ limes

1 bunch of fresh cilantro, chopped

1¼ teaspoon sea salt

Several grinds of black pepper

Mayonnaise, to serve (optional)

Two dozen slider buns

TO MAKE

1. Preheat the oven to 400°F.

2. Toss the shrimp with 2 tablespoons of the olive oil in a rimmed baking sheet, spread out evenly across the pan, and roast for 10 minutes. Let the shrimp cool for a few minutes, then slice each one in half down the center.

3. In a large bowl, combine the prepared shrimp, the crab, red pepper, cucumber, tomatoes, celery, pickles, the juice of 2 limes, half of the cilantro, 1 teaspoon of the sea salt, and the black pepper. Stir until all ingredients are fully combined. Store in the refrigerator until ready to serve.

4. At serving time, in a small bowl, toss the remaining cilantro with the remaining 1 tablespoon of olive oil, the juice from ¼ lime, and the remaining ¼ teaspoon sea salt.

5. Spread a little mayo on the bottom slider bun, if desired. Sprinkle a little cilantro salad over that. Spoon on some of the seafood mixture and then add the top bun.

6. Repeat until you have enough sliders for your picnic guests, or until it is all gone. «‹

⟫⟫ Fruta Picada

When I was pregnant, I nearly ate my weight in watermelon. Once, when I mentioned my recent hefty consumption of the watery fruit to a friend, right then and there, he introduced me to the glories of fruta picada, *bestowing my rotund, overheated self with a heaping plateful. A combination of fresh fruit, lime juice, and chili seasoning, this treat is served at markets and roadsides throughout Mexico. The combination of spice and salt partnered with sweet fruit is hard to beat on a warm summer's day.* SERVES 8 TO 10

YOU WILL NEED

for the spice blend

3 tablespoons chipotle powder

3 tablespoons smoky paprika

1 tablespoon plus 2 teaspoons sea salt

1 tablespoon cumin seeds

1½ teaspoons celery seeds

for the fruit mixture

1 pineapple, peeled, cored, and cut into spears

½ watermelon, peeled, cut into spears, and seeded

1 large jicama, peeled and cut into spears

1 large papaya, peeled, seeded, and cut into spears

Juice from 2 limes

TO MAKE

1. Grind all the spice blend ingredients together in a spice grinder or food processor or with a mortar and pestle until finely powdered. Transfer to a lidded container with a shaker screen.

2. Place all the fruit spears onto a serving platter. Squeeze the fresh lime juice evenly across. Let guests serve themselves as much fruit as they'd like and then sprinkle with the spice blend. ⟪⟪

Gingersnap *and* Coconut Lime Tassies

The combination of lime, ginger, and coconut is one of my favorites, and a perfect refresher on hot days. Here, the flavorful trinity is made manifest in miniature. Tassies are great beach and lakeside foods, as they can be grabbed up by hand, requiring no silverware or serving bowls. MAKES 3 DOZEN

YOU WILL NEED

for the crust

10 ounces gingersnaps

⅓ cup sweetened shredded coconut

6 tablespoons (¾ stick) salted butter, melted

for the filling

1 can (14 ounces) sweetened condensed milk

3 egg yolks, beaten

¼ cup fresh lime juice

Zest of 2 limes

TO MAKE

1. *Prepare the Crusts:* Preheat the oven to 350°F. Liberally coat 3 dozen mini muffin cups with nonstick cooking spray (I use coconut oil cooking spray). Alternatively, butter the muffin tins. Set aside.

2. Place the gingersnaps and coconut in a food processor. Pulse until the cookies are completely broken down into fine crumbs. Transfer to a medium bowl. Add the melted butter, and using clean hands or a metal mixing spoon, combine until the butter is fully incorporated.

3. Put a generous tablespoon of the mixture into each muffin tin. Press into the bottom and up the sides, using your fingers, a tart tamp, or a wooden handle such as that on a mojito muddler.

4. Bake for 10 minutes. Set aside to cool completely.

5. *Prepare the Filling:* Whisk all the filling ingredients together in a medium bowl.

6. Place 1 heaping tablespoon of filling atop each cooled tassie crust.

7. Bake at 350°F for 15 minutes. Allow to cool completely before serving. Tassies can be served chilled or at room temperature. ⫷

» lunch break «

PICNIC

Once upon a time, my most productive bouts of novel reading occurred over my lunch breaks. When I worked as a medical assistant and nutrition consultant four days a week, weather permitting, I'd take my lunch and a book and head outside. As the sun beat high and heavy in the sky, I'd find a shady spot beneath a small tree grove sited just outside the office building and settle in. During those precious thirty-minute breaks, I voraciously consumed the writings of Sue Monk Kidd, Jill McCorkle, Annie Dillard, Sarah Addison Allen, and so many others. A bit of food, some fresh air, and a relaxing read were all it took to regroup and renew.

A lunch break picnic is the perfect midday opportunity to shake up your routine. Some fresh air, good eats, and easy, stimulating yet relaxing activities will leave you feeling jazzed and invigorated for whatever the rest of the day brings. While wonderful enjoyed solo, this would also be a fun way to share a bit of the day with a spouse, significant other, family member, or coworker. You could even turn it into an ongoing, standing occasion for when the weather is nice. If it does end up just being you, though, bring along a good book. In no time you'll have worked your way through countless pages, too!

✳ to MAKE & DO

SELECT A SITE

Those working by the hour typically have lunch breaks running between thirty and sixty minutes long. With those time parameters in mind, you'll need to choose a picnicking location that's not terribly far from your workplace. For the picnic pictured, I chose a public green space in downtown Asheville, North Carolina, located just a few blocks away from the model's office. A similar, quickly reached destination would work wonderfully here.

GET PHYSICAL

Whether you're a chef or nurse, on your feet all the workday long or sitting in front of a computer from nine to five, come lunchtime, your lower body could use a bit of a workout. Gentle leg and foot stretches can make a world of difference in your productivity, and attitude, when you return to your post. No need to take your shoes off. Standing on tiptoe, pointing and flexing your feet while seated, or bending over to touch your toes—any of these will help increase circulation and relieve muscle fatigue.

CLOUD WATCHING

Some of my best ideas and bursts of creative inspiration come when I'm not thinking about anything in particular or trying to be creative at all. Cloud watching is one useful technique I sometimes employ when I want to empty my mind of cluttering thoughts and see what new, inspired ideas drift in. Consider looking to the skies during your Lunch Break Picnic.

TAKE PHOTOS

If you eat your lunch in the same location every day, it could be fun to bring along a camera to capture a daily image. Whether it's the same tree photographed each day, to note how it changes over the seasons, or something more spontaneous, like an unusual shadow or beautiful bird, grabbing a quick image can inject a bit of creativity and whimsy into your mealtime.

CONCOCT STORIES

Growing up, my mother was a huge fan of Simon and Garfunkel. I remember hearing the song "America" around age seven or eight and being particularly intrigued by several verses. The songwriters refer to two people's passing time together during a bus ride, playing a game where they create identities for their fellow travelers based on their faces. Ever since, I've loved to craft stories about strangers when sitting at a train station, on an airplane, or at an outdoor café. Consider letting your imagination run wild on your lunch break about the strangers in your midst. You'll pass the time and amuse yourself all at once!

to SAVOR & SIP

»» Rhubarb *and* Orange Chutney

I tend to think of chutney as a "bridge" condiment, representing the best of all offerings. A United Nations condiment, if you will, wherein sweet, sour, spicy, earthy, and crunchy are all accounted for. Slather a generous amount on some bread or crackers and pair with sharp cheddar and some salami for a simple yet satisfying main course. **MAKES 2½ PINTS**

YOU WILL NEED

for the spice bag

3 cardamom pods

½ teaspoon cumin seeds

½ teaspoon whole cloves

½ teaspoon whole yellow mustard seeds

1 teaspoon black peppercorns

1 teaspoon whole coriander seeds

½ cinnamon stick

for the chutney

2 cups chopped rhubarb stalks

1½ cups firmly packed light brown sugar

1 cup chopped sweet onions

⅓ cup raisins

2 garlic cloves, minced

2 teaspoons minced fresh ginger

1 cup apple cider vinegar

¼ cup orange liquor or juice

1 tablespoon orange zest

1 teaspoon ground cinnamon

¼ teaspoon ground cloves

2 teaspoons yellow mustard seeds

1 teaspoon pickling or kosher salt

TO MAKE

1. *Prepare the Spice Bag:* Place all the spice bag ingredients into a small muslin tea bag and cinch the top to close.

2. *Prepare the Chutney:* Put the spice bag, chopped rhubarb, brown sugar, onions, raisins, garlic, ginger, and vinegar into a large heavy stainless steel saucepan. Bring to a gentle boil over medium heat, then reduce the heat to low and simmer, uncovered, for 30 minutes. Add the orange liquor, orange zest, ground cinnamon, ground cloves, yellow mustard seeds, and salt. Simmer an additional 30 minutes, stirring frequently to prevent sticking. If more liquid is necessary, add water in ¼ cup increments.

3. When finished, remove the spice bag and set aside to compost the spices. Next, either fill half-pint jars and process them in a boiling water bath for 10 minutes (adjusting for altitude as needed), or store the chutney in a lidded container in the refrigerator and use within 3 weeks. »»

»» Deli-Style Spicy Mustard

I am an equal opportunity mustard lover. If presented with any incarnation of it, I will most certainly slather some on whatever I'm eating. This deli-style mustard is my homage to the spicy mustards available at nicer sandwich shops and delis. Bear in mind that it'll be rather robust at first, but will mellow considerably over time. MAKES ABOUT ¾ CUP

YOU WILL NEED

¼ cup whole yellow mustard seeds

2 tablespoons whole brown mustard seeds

1 teaspoon sea salt

1 teaspoon ground turmeric

Pinch of ground cloves

¾ cup apple cider vinegar

TO MAKE

1. Put the yellow and brown mustard seeds, salt, turmeric, and cloves into a food processor or blender. Process until the seeds begin to break down a bit.

2. Begin adding the vinegar, just a bit at a time, pulsing between additions. Once all the vinegar is added, process until the seeds are mostly broken open and a coarse paste forms.

3. Transfer the mustard to a glass or ceramic container. Cover with a lid and place in the refrigerator. The mixture will both thicken and mellow a bit in flavor as it sits, so plan to make the mustard several days before you intend to use it.

4. Store in the refrigerator and use within 3 or 4 weeks. «««

»» Carrot *and* Fennel Quick Pickle

On your lunch break, it can be enormously helpful to have something to eat that truly enlivens your senses, making you more alert and ready to power through the rest of the workday. These pickles deliver on that mission, and then some. They're lovely to behold, full of crunch and texture, highly flavorful, and heavy with aroma. If you come across orange, red, or yellow carrots, you've struck visual gold! MAKES 2 PINTS

YOU WILL NEED

1 cup water

1 cup apple cider vinegar

1 tablespoon pickling or kosher salt

1 tablespoon sugar

2 garlic cloves

2 teaspoons fennel seeds

1 teaspoon coriander seeds

1 teaspoon black peppercorns

1 teaspoon whole brown
   mustard seeds

³/₄ pound carrots, cut into
   2-inch spears

1 fennel bulb, cut into 2-inch spears
   (reserve fronds)

TO MAKE

1. Combine the water, vinegar, salt, sugar, garlic, fennel seeds, coriander seeds, peppercorns, and mustard seeds in a medium saucepan. Bring to a gentle boil over medium-high heat. Reduce heat to low and simmer for 5 minutes.

2. Remove the pan from the heat, cover with a lid, and set aside for 20 minutes.

3. Divide the carrot spears, fennel spears, and fennel fronds between two pint jars. Pour the spiced brine evenly over the vegetables, being careful to place 1 garlic clove into each jar along with the brine.

4. Cover the jars with lids and place in the refrigerator. Allow to infuse for at least 24 hours before serving, keeping in mind that the longer they infuse, the more developed the brine's flavor will become and the more intensely it will then transfer to the vegetables.

5. Store any unused portion in the refrigerator and use within 1 month. «««

» sacred tree «

PICNIC

Several years ago, when viewing James Cameron's film *Avatar*, I experienced a profound, visceral, emotional reaction to one of the scenes. The Na'vi, inhabitants of the film's fictitious moon Pandora, are gathered together around a sacred tree known to them as the Tree of Souls. Using their ability to directly communicate with the biological neural network that permeates all life on Pandora, the Na'vi join together to connect with their fellow inhabitants.

As I watched the scene unfold, I suddenly became aware of tears flowing freely down my cheeks and soft sobs coming from my throat. To me, trees have always been powerful and majestic and deserving of reverence and awe, no matter their size. They give so freely of their resources, providing for the needs of countless species. From carbon sequestration to shelter, food to fuel, trees give and give and give, even after their death.

With this picnic, I invite you to make a pilgrimage to a tree you consider "sacred." It could be one in your backyard; in an area park, botanical garden, or arboretum; deep in a forest; high atop a mountain—anywhere, really. The location isn't nearly as important as the significance. What does the tree mean to you and your fellow picnickers personally? Why does its presence speak to you? Were you married beneath it? Did you have your first kiss beside it? Or does its shape, or age, or girth evoke within you a sense of awe? Perhaps you simply find it lovely to behold.

For your picnic basket, I'm offering recipes that honor the foods trees provide. Pack up a feast, gather your loved ones, and head to your tree of choice. As you gather together to eat and play and explore beneath its branches, consider all the tree gives. You might be surprised with all you come up with. From nourishing our bodies to cooling our homes to tending to our souls, trees give unconditionally, and we would do well to steward and honor them in return.

✳ to MAKE & DO

SELECT A SITE

As mentioned previously, the location of the tree you intend to picnic beside isn't quite as significant as *why* you've chosen that particular tree. Is it where you got engaged? Made a new friend? Learned of a loved one's passing? Whiled away days as a child? Played on your grandmother's farm? What matters most here is that the tree feels meaningful and sacred to you and your guests.

HAIKU

Consider putting down in words your appreciation for the tree you're picnicking under. A Japanese style of poetry, haiku are short poems of seventeen *on*, or syllables, often divided into three phrases: five syllables, seven syllables, and five syllables (although it's not absolutely necessary to adhere strictly to that format). Penning a haiku collaboratively with your fellow picnickers, individually, or by electing whoever is deemed the day's "poet laureate" will do much to etch an indelible memory of the day.

GO OUT ON A LIMB

If the tree is in good enough shape to allow, and it's permissible to physically approach it, find your inner child and get climbing! Trees provide so very much, not the least of which is a great opportunity for exercise and exploration!

✳ to BEHOLD & EXPLORE

MAGNIFYING THE EXPERIENCE

Bring along a magnifying lens and get up close and personal with your specimen! Either a larger lens with a handle or a small doublet or even triplet handheld magnifier will reveal worlds of activity and information otherwise invisible to the naked eye.

TREE GIFTS

Depending on the tree you've chosen for your picnic, any number of "gifts" might be available to you. Nuts, pods, fruits, seeds, leaves, flowers, branches, and more may be on display during your visit. If you're able to do so without disturbing the tree, look for a takeaway "gift" to bring home. Those bits that have fallen off of their own accord are best, like gumballs, oak pods, black walnut hulls, acorns, leaves, and so on.

* to SAVOR & SIP *

››› Quinoa *and* Pecan Casserole

Quinoa is a small grain possessed of a wonderfully nutty flavor. It's also high in protein and other nutrients. I've partnered it here with nuts, mushrooms, and plenty of aromatics for a fragrant, robust, vegetarian entrée. Pecans grow abundantly on trees in the southeastern United States and are sometimes considered symbols of wealth. Here's to health, wealth, and all the best in life!

SERVES 8 TO 10

YOU WILL NEED

3 cups pecan pieces

2 cups uncooked quinoa

3 tablespoons olive oil

1 small onion, diced

1 red bell pepper, diced

3 garlic cloves, minced

1 pound crimini mushrooms, sliced

1 cup red wine

1 teaspoon dried thyme

1 teaspoon dried marjoram

1 teaspoon sea salt

Several grinds of black pepper

4 ounces grated Parmesan cheese

3 ounces Gruyère cheese

1 pound cottage cheese

6 eggs

¼ cup whole milk

Dash of hot sauce

TO MAKE

1. Butter a 9 × 13-inch baking pan and set aside.

2. Preheat the oven to 300°F. Spread the pecan pieces out on a rimmed baking sheet. Toast for 10 minutes, until fragrant. Set aside. Increase the heat to 350°F.

3. Bring 3 cups of water to a boil in a medium saucepan. Add the quinoa, cover with a lid, and reduce the heat to low. Simmer for 12 minutes, stirring every few minutes to prevent sticking.

4. While the quinoa cooks, warm the olive oil in a medium saucepan over medium-high heat. Add the onion and pepper and cook for about 8 minutes, until the vegetables are limp and slightly browned.

5. Add the garlic to the onion mixture and cook, stirring, for 1 minute.

6. Add the mushrooms and cook for about 15 minutes, until the liquid given off by the vegetables has fully evaporated.

7. Add the wine, thyme, marjoram, salt, and black pepper to the onion mixture, and stir to fully combine. Cook for about 15 minutes, until there is no more liquid in the pan.

8. Meanwhile, when the quinoa is done, remove from the heat, remove the lid, and fluff the grains well with a fork. Let sit for 3 to 4 minutes. Fluff the grains again and then stir in 3 ounces of the Parmesan and the Gruyère and cottage cheese. Transfer to a large bowl. Stir in the mushroom and onion mixture and roasted pecans.

continued

9. In a medium bowl, beat the eggs with the milk and hot sauce. Add to the quinoa and vegetable mixture, stirring until everything is fully incorporated.

10. Spoon the mixture into the prepared baking pan, and level the top.

11. Sprinkle the remaining 1 ounce of Parmesan over the top.

12. Bake for 1 hour, until the cheese has browned on top and the mixture has firmed up. Allow to cool for at least 15 minutes before serving. ⫷

»» Moroccan Apple Salad

Apples are perhaps the first things that come to mind when considering tree-grown edibles. They certainly were for me. Toss in some walnuts and a yogurt-based dressing, and you've got a delicious homage to arboreal eats! **SERVES 6 TO 8**

YOU WILL NEED

3 red apples, cored and roughly chopped (Gala, Fuji, Stayman Winesap, or Honeycrisp would all be lovely here)

1 cup diced celery

1 cup halved green grapes

½ cup currants

½ cup walnuts

½ cup whole fat Greek yogurt

1 tablespoon white wine vinegar

1 tablespoon fresh lemon juice

2 tablespoons finely chopped fresh mint

2 teaspoons ground coriander

½ teaspoon sea salt

TO MAKE

1. Put the apples, celery, grapes, currants, and walnuts in a medium bowl.

2. In a small bowl, whisk together the yogurt, vinegar, lemon juice, mint, coriander, and sea salt.

3. Pour the yogurt dressing over the apple mixture. Stir until everything is fully coated. Serve immediately, or store in a lidded container in the refrigerator and consume within 2 days. «««

⟫ Jallab

A popular refreshing beverage in the Middle East, jallab *is typically made by diluting the syrup of grape molasses, dates, and rose water with water, and serving it over ice with golden raisins and pine nuts. In my version, I'm subbing pomegranate juice concentrate, readily available at foreign foods stores as well as online. Pomegranates and pine nuts are both tree-derived foods, ideal to showcase at a picnic honoring trees!* MAKES 1 GALLON

YOU WILL NEED

1 cup warm water

¼ cup honey

3 quarts cold carbonated water

1 cup concentrated pomegranate juice

Golden raisins, to serve

Pine nuts, to serve

Ice, to serve

TO MAKE

1. In a small bowl, whisk the honey into the warm water until fully incorporated. Allow the mixture to cool for 15 minutes.

2. Place the cold carbonated water into a gallon-size pitcher or jar. Stir in the pomegranate concentrate and honey syrup until well combined.

3. Pour into 8-ounce glasses, over ice. Add a sprinkle of pine nuts and golden raisins to each glass. ⟪

⟫ Spiced Shortbread

While not typically the first foods associated with trees, a good number of spices come from them. Cloves are the aromatic flower buds of the Syzygium aromaticum tree, while nutmeg hails from several species of tree in the genus Myristica (along with mace). Be sure to give the dough plenty of time to chill after making it, as it tremendously helps the sliced dough to hold its form during baking.

MAKES 2 DOZEN

YOU WILL NEED

2 cups all-purpose flour

½ cup sugar

½ teaspoon sea salt

1 cup (2 sticks) butter, cut into chunks

½ teaspoon ground cloves

½ teaspoon ground nutmeg

TO MAKE

1. Pulse together the flour, sugar, and salt in a food processor.

2. Add the butter, cloves, and nutmeg. Pulse until the mixture begins to come together and hold its shape. This will take about 1 to 2 minutes, so don't worry if the mixture looks crumbly at first.

3. Divide the dough in half. Place one half onto a sheet of parchment paper. Shape it into a 6-inch-long log and roll it up in the parchment. Repeat with the second half of dough. Place both parchment-wrapped logs in the refrigerator and chill for 1 to 2 hours.

4. Preheat the oven to 300°F. Line two baking sheets with parchment paper or silicone baking mats.

5. Remove the dough logs from the refrigerator. Slice each log into 12 rounds about ½ inch thick and arrange on the prepared baking sheets.

6. Bake for about 30 to 35 minutes, until the edges just begin to brown.

7. Allow the cookies to cool 10 minutes on the baking sheet then transfer to the wire rack until completely cooled. Transfer to a lidded container. ⟪

» ephemerals «

PICNIC

In the spring of 2013, I received what might possibly be the most intriguing, most covetable invitation I've even been fortunate enough to acquire. Sent by fellow cookbook author Barbara Swell, it was a request to join her and a small group of other women for a "Ladies Lady Slipper Boozy Tea Party." A rare orchid native to the area, lady slippers are astonishingly gorgeous and just so happen to populate the woods behind Barbara's Asheville, North Carolina, home for but a few fleeting weeks each May. Each guest was asked to bring a dish from their garden or pantry to share. In ages spanning five decades, we took to the woods for conversation, food, and conviviality.

When creating the idea for a picnic shining a light on fleeting, ephemeral foods, Barbara and her orchids came to mind. She graciously, generously allowed me to use her woods as the staging ground for this picnic's photo shoot. While wild turkeys called (loudly!), we nibbled and chatted and searched the woods for lady slippers to sit among and admire (three highly rare albino specimens call this patch of land their home) and other lovely ephemeral objects to surround our picnic area.

In a time when it's possible to get pretty much anything you desire, whenever you want it, it can be deeply rewarding to plug into a rhythm more tethered to time and space and place. Whether it's lady slipper orchids or morels or nettles or wild violets or elderflower, or any other short-lived botanical or fungus you're viewing or consuming (or both!), considering the lessons offered by ephemeral objects can prove quite satisfying. In his poem "To the Virgins, to Make Much of Time," the poet Robert Herrick writes: "Gather ye rosebuds while ye may,/ Old time is still a-flying; / And this same flower that smiles today / Tomorrow will be dying." Pausing to enjoy and appreciate the here and now envelops us in the present and tunes our senses to what's in plain view—at least for the time being.

✳ *to* MAKE & DO

SELECT A SITE

The place you choose for this picnic should, by definition, be a place populated with some kind of ephemeral. For me, it was a forested patch of lady slippers. There is also an area near my home containing fields of wild pink flowers that bloom for a few weeks each spring. That would be another perfect setting for this picnic. The ideal location would be one filled with short-lived beauties—whether flowers or herbs or other botanical bits—that merit taking the time to view and relax by.

SCAVENGER HUNT

A "leave everything in its place" hunt can be a wonderful way of exploring. Either search as a group or give individual lists asking your fellow picnickers to find (but leave!) items they might encounter in your chosen setting. Some suggestions might include a medicinal plant, a wild culinary plant, moss, lichens, an aquatic plant, a reptile, a mammal, and a bird.

✳ *to* BEHOLD & EXPLORE

EPHEMERALS TABLEAU

Put together a little assemblage of gleaned ephemeral objects from your picnicking area, displaying them on a small tray or platter as a centerpiece. Collect only those things in abundance: acorns, rocks, mushrooms, common wildflowers, pods, branches, leaves, and other similar ephemera will be lovely to look at while eating and can later serve as mementos if displayed at home. There are a few things you'll always want to keep in mind when foraging, whether for decorative or edible specimens. Only gather a few items, so that others may forage and also to keep the plant from becoming overharvested. If there is only one plant or specimen in an area, leave it so that it can continue to grow. Last, harvest only the outermost leaves and a small percentage of the fruits and nuts of a plant, so that it can reproduce the following year.

MUSHROOM SPORE PRINT

Making a mushroom spore print, it seems as though you're witnessing magic unfold. It's both remarkably easy to do and profoundly thrifty to pull off. On your picnic, seek out a fresh mushroom, preferably one that has a wide, flat cap free of bruising or shriveling. When you return home, remove the stem from the cap. Place the cap with the spore side down on a piece of white paper. Cover the entire cap with a bowl or glass wide enough to fully enclose it. Leave overnight. Remove the bowl, gently remove the mushroom, and voilà! The mushroom's spores will have fallen from the mushroom and left a distinguishable print on the paper.

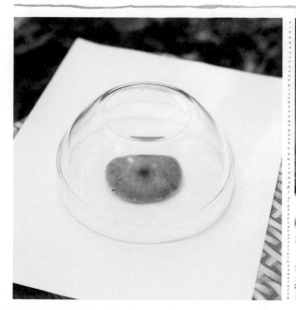

>>> Spring Onion *and* Chicken Liver Pâté

Chicken liver pâté is one of those dishes I had no idea I'd like so much until I got up the nerve to just try it already. Rich with fat and flavor, my version here includes spring onions and some aromatic herbs and spices to round out the characteristic "liver" taste. If you have any onion jelly on hand, or can add some sautéed onions to another type of jelly, it really does an expert job of complementing the pâté. **SERVES 6 TO 8**

YOU WILL NEED

2 tablespoons capers

¾ cup (1½ sticks) unsalted butter

3 spring onions, chopped into ¼-inch pieces, white and green parts kept separate

1 pound chicken livers (see Note)

1 cup white wine

½ teaspoon ground allspice

1 teaspoon thyme (fresh or dried)

1 teaspoon sea salt

Freshly ground black pepper

Fresh thyme leaves (optional)

TO MAKE

1. Sauté the capers in 2 tablespoons of the butter for 1 to 2 minutes, just until they start to brown. Remove the capers with a slotted spoon and set aside.

2. Add the white parts of the spring onions to the pan. Sauté over medium heat for 5 minutes, until slightly limp and fragrant. Add the green parts of the onions and cook for 5 more minutes. Remove all the onions from the pan, and set aside in a small bowl.

3. Add another 2 tablespoons of the butter to the pan, and add the livers. Cook until browned, about 5 minutes. Add the wine, allspice, thyme, salt, and pepper. Cook until all the liquid has evaporated.

4. Turn off the heat and stir in the onions. Let the mixture cool down for a few minutes, then transfer to a food processor. Pulse with another 4 tablespoons of the butter, 1 tablespoon at a time, until smooth.

5. Spoon the mixture into a small dish, then smooth it level with a spreader. Top it evenly with the sautéed capers and then gently press them about halfway into the pâté.

6. Melt the remaining 4 tablespoons of butter and spoon off some of the milk solids. Drizzle the melted butter over the top of the pâté until it is entirely sealed and covered evenly. Top with fresh thyme leaves if desired.

7. Chill for at least 2 hours. Serve with crackers or bread and onion jam or jelly with sautéed onions stirred into it.

Note: If you prefer a milder pâté, you can first soak the livers in a little bit of milk for 2 hours, then drain and proceed with the recipe. <<<

»» Nettle Pesto Pasta Salad

Stinging nettles are an early spring ephemeral. They can be harvested in the wild or found at area farmers' markets. Rich in minerals, stinging nettles are both beneficial to our bodies and delectable to our taste buds. Here I've rendered them into a fragrant pesto. When handling stinging nettles, whether you're the one harvesting or preparing, do be sure to follow the suggestion to wear rubber gloves. Tiny stickers on the underside of the leaves can be quite painful if allowed to make contact with skin. SERVES 6 TO 8

YOU WILL NEED

3 tablespoons plus 1 teaspoon sea salt

Loosely packed gallon bag of nettle leaves (see Note)

1 pound pasta, such as fusilli or torchiette

½ cup olive oil

1 garlic clove, loosely smashed

3 ounces hydrated sun-dried tomatoes

¼ cup pine nuts

½ cup grated Parmesan cheese

A few grinds of black pepper

Juice of ¼ lemon

2 dozen pitted green olives, sliced into thirds

¼ cup capers

TO MAKE

1. Fill a large stockpot about halfway with water. Add 3 tablespoons of the sea salt and bring to a boil. Meanwhile, soak the nettles in cool water for 5 minutes. Wearing rubber gloves, remove the leaves from the stems. Place the leaves into the pot of boiling water and boil vigorously for 1 minute.

2. Drain the nettles in a colander and spread the blanched leaves out across a cutting board. Leave to cool for 10 minutes and then dry them with a kitchen towel until most of the water is squeezed out. Chop coarsely and set aside.

3. Cook the pasta according to the instructions on the package.

4. Meanwhile, in a medium sauté pan, gently heat the olive oil with the smashed garlic clove until the garlic is golden brown. Remove the pan from the heat and discard the garlic. Set aside the pan of infused oil.

5. When the pasta is done, drain it in a colander, transfer to a large bowl, and stir the sun-dried tomatoes into it.

6. Pulse the nettles in a food processor with the pine nuts, Parmesan, pepper, lemon juice, and the remaining 1 teaspoon salt. Add the infused olive oil a little at a time, pulsing until smooth. Add a little extra olive oil if needed, to achieve your desired pesto consistency.

7. Add the pesto to the pasta and toss with the olives and capers until it is evenly coated. If not serving right away, transfer to a lidded container and store in the refrigerator. Bring to room temperature prior to serving.

Note: Handle the nettles with rubber kitchen gloves until they are cooked. ««

Swedish Crèmes *with* Rhubarb Compote

Years ago, I was introduced to Swedish crèmes, and ever since they have gone into my dessert Hall of Fame. This is my attempt at re-creating the creamy, sweet treat, topped off with a sour rhubarb compote to temper all that sweetness! **MAKES 6 HALF-PINT SERVINGS**

YOU WILL NEED

for the compote

1½ pounds rhubarb stalks, chopped

½ cup sugar

Juice and zest of 1 orange

¼ teaspoon ground allspice

for the crèmes

1 tablespoon gelatin

¼ cup cold water

2 cups heavy cream

¾ cup sugar

2 cups sour cream

2 teaspoons vanilla extract

TO MAKE

1. *Make the Compote:* Place the all the compote ingredients in a medium saucepan. Bring to a boil over high heat.

2. Reduce the temperature to low and simmer gently for 10 minutes, until the rhubarb has broken down a good bit and thickened.

3. Remove the pan from the heat, transfer the mixture to a glass or ceramic bowl, and cover with a lid. Store in the refrigerator until ready to top the crèmes.

4. *Make the Crèmes:* In a small mixing bowl, gently whisk together the gelatin and cold water. Leave for 1 minute.

5. Place the heavy cream, sugar, and gelatin mixture into a medium saucepan. Warm over medium heat for 4 to 5 minutes, stirring gently until the gelatin has fully dissolved. Remove the pan from the heat.

6. Transfer the mixture to a glass or ceramic bowl. Leave to cool for 20 minutes.

7. Whisk in the sour cream and vanilla extract until fully combined.

8. Divide the mixture evenly among 6 half-pint jars. Place in the refrigerator and leave to chill for 4 hours.

9. To serve, top each jar with a generous amount of compote, around ¼ to ⅓ cup. Store any unused portion, covered, in the refrigerator, and use within 1 or 2 days. ⟪

»» afternoon tea ««

PICNIC

The English tradition of taking an afternoon tea, replete with refreshments and sweet and savory bites to bridge the gap between lunch and dinner, is one I can seriously get behind. A lifelong grazer when it comes to eating, taking an afternoon break to refresh and renew is so attractive to me. The fact that doing so will help prevent plummeting blood sugar and its attendant "hangry" demeanor (for which I am sometimes known, unfortunately, by my sweet husband) endears it to me even more.

As a child, I hosted countless tea parties. Whether the guests in attendance included my parents, my brother, close friends, or a medley of much-loved stuffed animals, there was always a good deal of formality involved, so much as a young girl can be formal. Proper diction, good posture, and polite conversation were givens, naturally. A fair amount of queries beginning with "My dear lady" or "Good sir" were voiced. I really had no idea what I was doing, but I was having a wonderful time doing it.

Of course, there were also always a variety of things to sip and nibble at these afternoon teas. As I grew older and began experimenting with baking and cooking, the options moved from the store-bought to the homemade. Not every attempt was a success. There were horrific petit fours and dry brownies. But as I practiced, I gained confidence, and was eventually able to offer my guests treats they actually enjoyed consuming, without having to pretend.

Taking afternoon tea in picnic form removes a bit of the fussiness of indoor dining. The wind blows where it pleases, the ants crawl where they wish. All the better for a tea, I say. Put out your spread, pour yourself and your guests a spot of tea, sit back, and relax. Spirits will be invigorated, physical needs will be met, and the time in between meals will feel like a gift, not a burden.

SELECT A SITE

Find a grassy patch, well-appointed bench, or, in my case, a gazebo in a botanical garden. Any scenic setting that's not too difficult to reach (you're likely to have fragile teacups in tow!) would work well here. An added bonus would be a quiet area, to create an atmosphere of teatime tranquility.

CARD GAMES

Extremely compact and highly portable, a deck of cards is an ideal accompaniment to picnic activities. From Rummy to Spades to the all-ages Go Fish, there's a card game for every size of picnic and every gaming inclination. If you have four picnickers (and the knowledge for playing the game), Bridge would be a fine fit for an Afternoon Tea Picnic.

DRESS UP

An afternoon tea is a fantastic opportunity for donning a bit of finery. From dresses, gloves, and heels to bow ties, vests, and hats, this picnic is a chance for you and your guests to make the specialness of the occasion manifest in all arenas, including food, festivities, and frocks.

TEA-LEAF READING

Tasseography is the name ascribed to the art of reading tea leaves. A person skilled in this practice makes interpretations and predictions based on the natural arrangement of tea leaves on the bottom and sides of an emptied cup. Either inviting an individual who can perform tea-leaf readings or having an interpreting book on hand at this picnic would inject a bit of whimsy and mystique into the gathering. From what I've read on the subject, be forewarned that the interpretation by the reader is highly influenced by whatever spiritual traditions or practices to which he or she might already ascribe.

TEA IDENTIFICATION

Tea is the star of this picnic. It could be fun to test the extent of you and your guests' tea knowledge with a blind aroma identification. Steep individual bags or loose bits of however many teas you'd like. Place them on a small plate or serving platter. Whoever is administering the test should note to themselves which tea is which. Then, pass the plate and see if others can identify the tea by sight and aroma only. Whoever guesses all selections correctly could be given a package of tea as a prize.

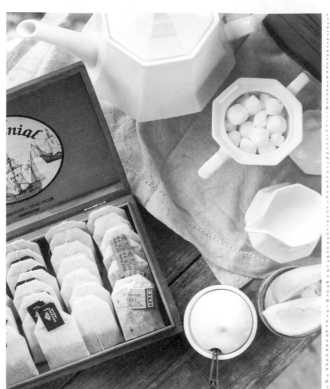

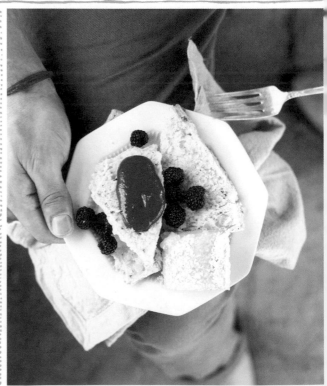

✳ to SAVOR & SIP ✳

»» Curried Egg Salad Cucumber Cups

While an avid fan of egg salad, I find some incarnations of it to be bland and one-note. Here I've upped the flavor via curry powder, cumin, and a small dollop of chutney. Egg salad gets tucked into cucumber-round cups, offering up a perfect bite of creaminess and crunch, all at once.

MAKES ABOUT 2 DOZEN

YOU WILL NEED

6 hard-boiled eggs

¼ cup mayonnaise

1 tablespoon lemon juice

1 teaspoon curry powder

½ teaspoon ground cumin

½ teaspoon sea salt

2 to 3 cucumbers, cut into ¾-inch-thick slices

¼ cup chutney, to serve (see Note)

TO MAKE

1. Chop the eggs into pea-size pieces. Put into a medium bowl and add the mayonnaise, lemon juice, curry powder, cumin, and salt.

2. With a melon baller, hollow out each cucumber slice, leaving just a thin layer at the bottom.

3. Put about a tablespoon of egg salad into each cucumber cup, until all of it has been used.

4. Top each cucumber cup with I teaspoon of chutney.

Note: You can use any flavor of chutney here. The Rhubarb and Orange Chutney (page 81) pairs especially well with the curried egg salad. «««

»» Smoked Salmon *and* Herb Finger Sandwiches

The smoky, salty creaminess of smoked salmon is a perfect foil for the sweetness of tea. Cradled between bread slices and topped with herb-riddled chèvre, it makes this sandwich a sophisticated yet unintimidating teatime delight. **MAKES ABOUT 2 DOZEN**

YOU WILL NEED

8 ounces chèvre, at
   room temperature

1 cup chopped fresh cilantro
   and fresh parsley, mixed

1 tablespoon Worcestershire sauce

Juice of ¼ lemon

Several grinds of black pepper

Loaf of sliced bread

¼ cup capers

Lox (smoked salmon)

TO MAKE

1. In a medium bowl, combine the chèvre, chopped herbs, Worcestershire sauce, lemon juice, and pepper.

2. Cut the crusts off the bread slices, then cut the slices in half, into rectangles.

3. Smear one side of all the bread slices with the herbed cheese. Sprinkle a few capers atop half of the slices, top each of these with a layer of lox, and then top them with another slice, cheese side down.

4. On a cutting board, cut the sandwiches diagonally, into triangles, then plate. «‹

Cordon Bleu Crostini

This is my teatime take on a cordon bleu sandwich. Crostini rounds are topped with roasted chicken, Emmenthaler cheese, and country ham crumbles. **MAKES ABOUT 1½ DOZEN**

YOU WILL NEED

for the filling

1½ pounds boneless, skinless chicken thighs

2 tablespoons olive oil

1 teaspoon sea salt

Several grinds of black pepper

¼ cup mayonnaise

2 tablespoons Dijon mustard

4 ounces country ham

for the crostini

1 baguette

Enough olive oil to coat a large baking pan

1 whole garlic clove, peeled (optional)

for the topping

3 ounces Emmenthaler, Swiss, or Gouda cheese, cut into thin 2-inch long strips

TO MAKE

1. *Prepare the Filling:* Preheat the oven to 350°F.

2. On a rimmed baking sheet, toss the chicken thighs in the olive oil. Sprinkle with salt and pepper and roast for 40 minutes until cooked through.

3. Let the chicken cool for at least 10 minutes, then chop finely or pulse in a food processor. Transfer the chopped chicken to a medium bowl. Stir in the mayonnaise and mustard.

4. Meanwhile, grill the country ham in a heavy pan till cooked through, and set aside to cool.

5. *Prepare the Crostini:* Turn the oven up to 400°F.

6. Cut the baguette into ¼-inch slices.

7. Liberally coat a rimmed baking sheet with olive oil. Place the baguette slices on the pan, pressing down on them gently. Turn the slices over and wiggle them a bit to help them absorb the olive oil on the other side. Bake for 12 minutes.

8. Remove the pan from the oven and rub one side of each crostini with the clove of garlic, if desired.

9. *Assemble the Sandwiches:* Spoon about a tablespoon of the chicken mixture onto each crostini. Chop the country ham into small slivers, and sprinkle some on top of each one. Top with a couple slices of the cheese and serve. ‹‹‹

Hazelnut *and* Nutmeg Scones *with* Raspberry Curd

In my mid-twenties, I worked in the production-bakery kitchen of a large natural foods store. Alongside baking biscuits, muffins, quick breads, and cookies, I was in charge of crafting scones. All that time spent baking them resulted in my becoming quite specific about what constitutes a good scone. Buttery but not doughy, with a pillowy interior and a toothsome crunch to the crust means a flawless scone to me. This version includes hazelnuts and nutmeg partnered with raspberry curd, but you could easily substitute whatever roasted nuts and spices you have on hand. Do slather on the curd liberally. We all know that's what everyone wants to do with fresh curd anyway. SERVES 8

YOU WILL NEED

for the curd

3 cups fresh raspberries

⅓ cup sugar

4 tablespoons (½ stick) unsalted butter, cubed

1 tablespoon plus 2 teaspoons fresh lemon juice

2 eggs

2 egg yolks

for the scones

2 cups all-purpose flour

3 tablespoons sugar

1 tablespoon baking powder

½ teaspoon sea salt

½ teaspoon ground nutmeg

5 tablespoons salted butter, cubed

¼ cup roasted and chopped hazelnuts

1 cup heavy cream

TO MAKE

1. *Prepare the Curd:* Using either a food processor or a blender, puree the berries. Place a fine-mesh sieve over a medium bowl and strain the berry puree. You may need to periodically swirl a small spoon or a clean finger through the sieve to release the puree into the bowl below. Set the strained-off seeds aside to compost.

2. You should end up with around 1½ cups of strained puree. If you have more than that, set aside the additional amount for another use.

3. Warm the puree, sugar, and butter in a medium saucepan over medium-high heat. Whisk in the lemon juice.

4. In a separate medium bowl, whisk together the eggs and egg yolks. Remove ½ cup of the warm puree from the saucepan and whisk it into the eggs. Return the mixture to the saucepan on the stove.

5. Turn the heat to low and cook, whisking constantly, until the curd begins to thicken. Remove the saucepan from the heat.

6. Transfer the curd to a glass or ceramic bowl. Cover with a lid and refrigerate 4 to 6 hours, until completely cooled and thickened.

continued

7. *Make the Scones:* Preheat the oven to 375°F. Line a rimmed baking sheet with a silicone baking mat or parchment paper and set aside.

8. In a medium bowl, sift together the flour, sugar, baking powder, salt, and nutmeg.

9. Using a pastry cutter or two forks, cut in the butter cubes until the mixture resembles coarse meal. Stir in the hazelnuts.

10. Add the heavy cream and stir gently with a mixing spoon just until the liquid is absorbed.

11. Turn the mixture out onto a lightly floured surface. Push it together with your hands until all the ingredients are fully combined. Form the dough into a circle 8 inches wide and about 1 inch thick. Cut into 8 wedges (a pastry dough bench cutter is very helpful for making clean lines in the dough).

12. Place the wedges on the lined baking sheet. Bake for 25 to 30 minutes, until golden on top. Let cool for 10 minutes on the baking sheet, then transfer to a cooling rack to cool completely. «

Rosemary Lemon Bars

I like a lemon bar that isn't timid, the kind where your salivary glands immediately go into overdrive at the first bite. Rosemary added to the crust adds a bit of unexpected intrigue and tempers all that puckery goodness. Take my word for it: you won't be able to stop at just one. **SERVES 16**

YOU WILL NEED

for the crust

1 cup all-purpose flour

¼ cup cornstarch

½ cup powdered sugar

½ teaspoon sea salt

½ cup (1 stick) plus 2 tablespoons unsalted butter, cubed

1 tablespoon minced fresh rosemary

for the filling

4 eggs

1 cup sugar

1 tablespoon fresh lemon zest

⅔ cup fresh lemon juice

¼ cup all-purpose flour

¼ teaspoon sea salt

TO MAKE

1. *Prepare the Crust:* Line either an 8 × 8-inch or a 9 × 9-inch baking pan with aluminum foil, allowing a 1-inch overhang of foil on all sides. Set aside.

2. Pulse the flour, cornstarch, powdered sugar, and salt in a food processor to combine. Add in the butter and rosemary and pulse until the butter and dry ingredients begin to come together.

3. Press the mixture into the prepared pan, pushing it fully into the corners and about ½ inch up the sides. Place in the refrigerator to chill for 30 minutes.

4. Preheat the oven to 350°F. Bake the crust for 20 to 25 minutes, until golden. Remove from the oven and set aside to cool briefly while you prepare the filling. Reduce the oven temperature to 325°F.

5. *Prepare the Filling:* Place all filling ingredients in a large bowl. Beat with an electric mixer until fully combined.

6. Pour the filling into the prepared crust (it's fine if the crust is still warm). Bake for 25 to 30 minutes, until the filling has fully set and doesn't jiggle when the pan is touched. Remove from the oven and set aside. Allow to cool fully.

7. Gently lift opposite sides of the foil overhang and place the entire square onto a cutting board. Slide a spatula between the foil and the bottom of the crust. Carefully lift the square and remove the foil from beneath it. Cut into 16 individual squares. If not serving immediately, keep refrigerated until serving time. ⫷

» romantic «

PICNIC

I am a hopeless romantic. So is my husband, Glenn. We love a sweet, happy ending and a loving resolution, whether in film, literature, or real life. Our own courtship was incredibly brief, with an engagement at our two-week mark and a marriage after five months. We both enjoy reading research and studies about what seems to aid in successful and long-lived relationships, as well as those things that purportedly bring about their demise. Innate matchmakers, we also enjoy trying to set up friends on dates, or simply discussing anything related to relationships, love, and life.

So when our dear friends Rob and Karie, co-owners of the Asheville-based design business Shelter Collective, became engaged and started seeking out possible wedding locations, offering our property as a potential site was our natural inclination. After all, it's where we exchanged our own vows back in June 2007. It also seemed natural to feature them in this romantic-themed picnic, in the very spot in which they would soon be exchanging vows and rings.

I hope that you will have the exquisite pleasure of experiencing a romantic picnic at some point in your life. Perhaps you already have. While all picnics are wonderful, one that focuses squarely on you and your beloved is a magical thing, indeed. Your senses are already heightened, courtesy of amorous feelings, so food and scenery can't help but be that much more intoxicating and satisfying.

✳ to MAKE & DO

SELECT A SITE

If you want to kindle romantic feelings or ignite existing passions, a beautiful location certainly can expedite those sentiments. A scenic park, mountaintop view, forested clearing, or other setting that inspires awe and where beauty abounds is key for this picnic.

FEED EACH OTHER

There's a reason brides and grooms traditionally feed each other pieces of wedding cake. Feeding ourselves is something we are totally capable of doing on our own as adults. The act of feeding another is a strong indicator of trust. It's a very intimate act, and it implies that complete confidence in the intentions of the other exists. It's also really fun and silly to do.

✳ to BEHOLD & EXPLORE

MAKE DAISY CHAINS

There is something so kind and gentle in crafting daisy chains. Wherever you might be picnicking, seek out a small handful of daisies together. Look for those with long stalks. Pick about 6 to 8 daisies, stems included. Once collected, use your thumbnail to split the stalk about halfway down its length. Next, thread the stalk of another daisy through this hole. Continue to repeat this process until a chain is created that is long enough to be worn either as a crown or as a necklace, and place it on your beloved.

* to SAVOR & SIP *

⟫⟫⟫ Roasted Figs *with* "Little Worlds"

Fresh figs are delicious, but roasted figs? Well, they're pretty much divine, in my estimation. Topped with what a friend referred to as "little worlds" of chèvre and fresh herbs, these simple hors d'oeuvres are sure to please. **MAKES 2 DOZEN**

YOU WILL NEED

3 ounces chèvre,
   at room temperature

2 dozen fresh mint leaves,
   finely chopped

1 dozen fresh figs, black or green
   or a combination

¼ cup olive oil

¼ cup balsamic vinegar,
   preferably white

1 teaspoon sea salt

2 tablespoons pistachios,
   finely crushed

TO MAKE

1. The night before serving, put the chèvre into a small bowl. Add the chopped mint and stir until evenly incorporated. Put into the refrigerator and chill overnight.

2. Preheat the oven to 450°F. Cut the figs in half, lengthwise, creating 24 portions.

3. Put the oil, vinegar, and salt into a lidded jar, cover tightly, and shake until fully combined.

4. Place the fig halves on a rimmed baking sheet. Pour the vinaigrette over them and gently toss to coat, then space them evenly across the pan, cut side up. Sprinkle the crushed pistachios evenly over the figs. Roast in the oven for 8 minutes.

5. Let the figs cool to room temperature, then place them on a serving plate.

6. Between your two palms, roll marble-size balls of the chilled cheese mixture. Gently place one ball on top of each fig half. The cheese balls turn out best if you wipe off your palms after rolling each ball. Also, try not to overwork the cheese when forming into rounds, as the heat of your hands will start to make them too soft. ⟪⟪⟪

⟫ Trout Salad *with* Crostini

So often, fish-based dips and spreads are overly laden with creaminess. Not that there's anything inherently wrong with creamy foods, but combined with seafood, dairy tends to overwhelm. Here I'm offering a vinaigrette-dressed dip. Fluffy, light, and beautiful, this dip transports well and is a great complement to the crunch of the crostini. SERVES 4

YOU WILL NEED

for the dip

¼ cup olive oil

1 tablespoon red wine vinegar

1 tablespoon coarse Dijon mustard

Pinch of sea salt

Several grinds of black pepper

8 ounces smoked trout or smoked salmon, cut into bite-size pieces

¼ cup diced pimentos

12 cornichons, sliced into thin discs

2 tablespoons capers

1 tablespoon currants

1 tablespoon fresh thyme leaves, stems removed

1 tablespoon fresh marjoram leaves, stems removed

1 hard-boiled egg, chopped into small pieces

for the crostini

1 baguette

Enough olive oil to coat a large baking pan

1 whole garlic clove, peeled (optional)

TO MAKE

1. *Prepare the Dip:* Put the olive oil, vinegar, mustard, salt, and pepper into a lidded jar, cover tightly, and shake until fully incorporated. Put the trout into a medium bowl and add the pimentos, cornichons, capers, currants, thyme, and marjoram and toss. Pour the vinaigrette over and toss to coat.

2. Put the bowl into the refrigerator and chill until serving time, at least 1 hour. Transfer to a serving bowl. Top with the chopped egg before serving.

3. *Prepare the Crostini:* Preheat the oven to 400°F.

4. Cut the baguette into ¼-inch slices.

5. Liberally coat a rimmed baking sheet with olive oil. Place the baguette slices on the pan, pressing down on them gently. Turn the slices over and wiggle them a bit to help them absorb the olive oil on the other side. Bake for 12 minutes.

6. Remove the pan from the oven and rub one side of each crostini with the clove of garlic, if desired. ⟪

»» Israeli Couscous Feta *and* Herb Salad

Round and fluffy, Israeli couscous is the gregarious cousin to the smaller, grainier couscous many are accustomed to. It is soft and tender and makes for a truly lovely salad when imbued with herbs and vegetables and seasonings (including basil, a claimed aphrodisiac). The salad is best eaten within 1 or 2 days of preparation, as its tender qualities generally don't hold up too well to moisture.

SERVES 4 TO 6

YOU WILL NEED

1¾ cups water

¼ cup plus 1 tablespoon olive oil

1⅓ cups uncooked Israeli couscous

1 medium cucumber

4 ounces feta cheese, crumbled

2 medium tomatoes, chopped into small bite-size pieces

2 dozen fresh basil leaves, cut in chiffonade

1 dozen fresh mint leaves, cut in chiffonade

Several grinds of black pepper

2 tablespoons red wine vinegar

½ teaspoon sea salt

TO MAKE

1. Bring the water to a boil. While it heats, warm 1 tablespoon of the olive oil in a medium saucepan over medium-high heat. Add the couscous and sauté until lightly browned, about 5 minutes. Pour in the boiling water slowly, stirring to incorporate.

2. Reduce the heat to low, cover, and simmer for about 11 to 12 minutes. Stir the couscous, fluffing it up with a spoon or fork. Set aside to cool to room temperature.

3. Meanwhile, peel the cucumber, cut off the ends, and cut it in half lengthwise. Using a spoon or melon baller, scoop out the seeds, then cut the pieces in half lengthwise again. Cut the cucumber spears into segments about ⅛ inch thick.

4. Transfer the cooled couscous to a mixing bowl. Add the feta, tomatoes, cucumbers, basil, mint, and pepper to the couscous and toss.

5. Put the remaining ¼ cup olive oil, vinegar, and salt into a lidded jar and cover tightly. Shake vigorously to fully combine, and then pour over the couscous and vegetable mixture and toss. Serve at room temperature. «««

»» Pots de Crème *with* Rose Whipped Cream

I enjoy chocolate as much as the next person, but I don't pine or clamor for it in the way that some do. That said, if I see pots de crème *on a menu or in a bakery's dessert case, I'll likely end up choosing it. Smooth, creamy, and intensely decadent, only a little is needed of this luscious dessert to satisfy your sweet tooth. A long purported aphrodisiac, chocolate contains phenylalanine, an amino acid that triggers dopamine and serotonin, neurotransmitters that regulate and enhance mood. Add in a bit of rose water—infused whipped cream, and you're on your way to a loving high in no time!* SERVES 6

YOU WILL NEED

for the pots de crème

1 cup milk

¾ cup heavy cream

3 egg yolks, at room temperature

⅓ cup sugar

1 teaspoon vanilla extract

Pinch of sea salt

4 ounces dark chocolate, chopped (65% cocoa content or higher)

for the whipped cream

1 cup heavy cream

1 tablespoon powdered sugar

1 teaspoon rose water

Raspberries, to serve

TO MAKE

1. Put on a kettle of water to boil while you prepare the *pots de crème*. Preheat the oven to 325°F. Line the bottom of a high-sided baking pan with a kitchen cloth. Set six 4-ounce ramekins or cups atop the kitchen cloth. Set aside.

2. Warm the milk and cream in a medium saucepan, just to the point of bubbles breaking the surface. Remove the pan from the heat.

3. In a medium bowl, whisk together the egg yolks, sugar, vanilla, and salt.

4. Place the chopped chocolate in a heatproof bowl. Slowly pour the warmed milk over the chocolate. Leave it to sit for 1 to 2 minutes, then whisk until the chocolate is fully melted.

5. Slowly whisk the egg yolk mixture into the chocolate mixture, beating until fully combined.

6. Divide the mixture evenly among the six ramekins. Pour the boiling water into the pan, until the water comes halfway up the sides of the ramekins (this creates a bain-marie, or water bath, that will gently steam the *pots de crème* as they bake).

7. Bake for 25 to 30 minutes, until the centers of the *pots de crème* don't jiggle when touched. Remove the pan from the oven. Remove the ramekins from the pan and set on a wire cooling rack until they reach room temperature. Transfer to the refrigerator to chill for at least 4 hours before serving.

8. At serving time, beat together the heavy cream, powdered sugar, and rose water until soft peaks form and the cream sticks to the back of a spoon. Dollop liberally onto the *pots de crème* and top with fresh raspberries, if desired. ««

»» movie night ««

PICNIC

My older brother, Jimmy, his wife, Emily, and their young sons live in Charlotte, North Carolina, about a two-and-a-half-hour drive from my home in the mountains. Several times a year, we make the trip down for my nephews' birthdays or other family gatherings. About midway through the drive, on an otherwise desolate stretch of four-lane highway leading into the town of Shelby, we pass the Sunset Drive-In Theater. Although I've yet to watch a film there (we're always on our way elsewhere), just the sight of a drive-in movie theater elicits intense memories.

I was born in the summer of 1976, well before the days of high-definition films and surround-sound theaters with stadium-style seating and reclining chairs with plush cushions and built-in cupholders. Many magical movies made their debut in the ensuing years, including *Star Wars*, *E.T.*, and *Raiders of the Lost Ark*. During those days, my older brother and I were quite young, around two and four years old. Seeking out creative ways to keep two toddlers happy and occupied for a few hours, my father would pack us into his car and head to the local drive-in theater to take in a movie.

I have no doubt that the film quality at Sunset Drive-In leaves much to be desired. The sound is likely scratchy and warbled, too. When viewing a movie at the drive-in, however, none of that really matters. The lure of such a setting isn't the stellar cinematic experience. It's the pleasure of being outdoors, and for me, it's the nostalgia of being young and carefree and in the company of a loving parent. Under the canopy of the stars, subject to the elements, in tune to the sights and smells and sounds of the greater, wide world, that's where the magic happens, for me and for many others.

At this picnic, comfort is key. Spread out as many blankets and pillows as you are in possession of (and if it turns out you lack some, ask your guests to bring along some of their own). Cozy down with beverages (I made homemade root beer for the occasion using the recipe from my beverage book, *Quench*) and handheld savory eats and treats, and get ready to enjoy the splendor to be experienced at the intersection of the night sky and outdoor movie.

✶ to MAKE & DO

SELECT A SITE

The ideal location for this picnic is a private backyard. That way there will be easy access to electric outlets for the projector and speakers, grassy lawns for comfy lounging, and a reduced likelihood of auditory interference from other people or pets. The film can be projected onto the side of a house, an outdoor structure such as a garage or shed, or onto a sheet over a clothesline.

MENU MATCHING

It could be fun to play around with matching the movie to the menu at this picnic. The recipes I'm offering here are more "all-around cinematic" in nature, but crafting a menu inspired by your chosen film is another option. French foods for an *Amélie* viewing, a Greek feast for a showing of *Mamma Mia!*, or homemade Baby Ruths to enjoy during *Goonies* are some ideas to consider.

PAJAMA TIME

Since this picnic invites lounging on blankets and pillows at night, cozying up in pajamas come movie time completely makes sense. Have guests either arrive in pj's or change into them once they arrive. Little children often fall asleep during films, anyway, so their jammy-clad status will be that much more agreeable to their parents for the trip home and transfer to bed at night's end.

✶ to BEHOLD & EXPLORE

FILM CHARADES

Before the movie begins, it could be fun to engage in a bit of cinematic charades. Choose one person to silently act out characters, scenes, or aspects of famous, well-known films. Only hand gestures and pantomiming can be used to offer clues. Movies to consider include *Gone with the Wind*, *Star Wars*, *The Wizard of Oz*, *E.T.*, *The Lord of the Rings* movies, and many, many others. If the crowd includes a good amount of children, the adults might want to cater the films to them. Otherwise, anything goes!

to SAVOR & SIP

»» Rosemary *and* Parmesan Popcorn

Fresh rosemary, Parmesan cheese, and corn are delicious in creamy polenta, so it occurred to me they'd marry equally well in a savory popcorn. I'm so glad I wagered such a guess, because boy, was I ever correct! The children present for this picnic were wowed by a newfangled version of a beloved treat (always a good sign!), and the adults positively gobbled it up. Best of all, it's ready to serve in about 5 minutes. **MAKES 8 CUPS**

YOU WILL NEED

2 large fresh rosemary sprigs

8 cups popped popcorn

¼ cup grated Parmesan cheese

2 to 3 teaspoons sea salt, to taste

TO MAKE

1. Remove the needles from the rosemary sprigs. Set aside the stems to compost. Finely mince the needles.

2. Combine the popcorn, prepared rosemary, Parmesan, and salt in a large bowl. Using clean hands or a large metal spoon, toss to fully incorporate all the ingredients and serve. «««

≫ Salted Caramel Popcorn

This is my grown-up take on Cracker Jack, that iconic cinema treat of days long past. Here the cloy-ing sweetness often associated with caramel corn is balanced by sea salt. This is a treat best shared, as it's entirely possible to eat it all without realizing you've done so (it's that good!). MAKES 8 CUPS

YOU WILL NEED

8 cups popped popcorn

1 cup sugar

½ cup (1 stick) butter, melted

½ cup maple syrup

1 tablespoon sea salt

1 cup roasted peanuts (optional)

TO MAKE

1. Preheat the oven to 350°F.

2. Melt the sugar in a medium saucepan over medium-low heat, stirring frequently, until all the granules are melted and the color just begins to turn copper.

3. Carefully stir in the butter. Stir in the maple syrup, and keep stirring until the mixture achieves a uniform consistency.

4. Divide the popcorn between two large, rimmed baking sheets. Toss with the sea salt. Add the peanuts, if desired.

5. Evenly drizzle the caramel over both trays of popcorn, tossing with tongs to incorporate.

6. Bake for 15 minutes. Switch the baking sheets to opposite oven racks and bake for 10 more minutes.

7. Allow the caramel corn to cool on the pans a bit, then break it up into a bowl and serve. ≪

Mini Sausage *and* Leek Calzones *with* Fresh Tomato Dipping Sauce

Much like pizza, calzones are often associated with movie viewing. Both can be a bit messy, though, so I've streamlined things and created a mini calzone. Easily portable, handheld, and tasty served warm or at room temperature, these are sure to please. **MAKES 2 DOZEN**

YOU WILL NEED

for the dipping sauce

3 tablespoons olive oil, plus a drizzle

1 medium onion, diced

3 garlic cloves, minced

3 pounds fresh tomatoes, diced

1 tablespoon sugar

1 teaspoon sea salt

Several grinds of black pepper

3 tablespoons tomato paste

½ cup lightly packed grated Parmesan cheese

2 tablespoons chopped fresh marjoram

1 tablespoon chopped fresh thyme

continued

TO MAKE

1. *Prepare the Dipping Sauce:* Warm 3 tablespoons of olive oil in a medium saucepan over medium-high heat. Add the onions and sauté for 10 minutes. Add the garlic. Cook, stirring frequently, for 1 to 2 minutes, then add the tomatoes, sugar, salt, and pepper.

2. Simmer for 45 minutes, stirring regularly to prevent sticking. Stir in the tomato paste. Cook for 15 more minutes, then stir in the Parmesan and remove from the heat.

3. Stir in the marjoram and thyme and drizzle with olive oil.

4. *Prepare the Filling:* Cut the leeks into ½-inch rings. Wash the leek rings in a bowl of cold water, removing any dirt or debris. Gently pat dry with a kitchen cloth.

5. Warm 2 tablespoons of the olive oil in a medium saucepan over medium-high heat. Add the leeks and sauté for about 10 minutes, until they start to brown a little around the edges.

6. Add 1 cup of the wine and the stock and brown sugar. Reduce the heat to low and simmer, stirring occasionally, for about 25 minutes, until the liquid has evaporated and the leeks are golden brown. Remove the leeks from the pan and set aside.

7. Add the remaining 2 tablespoons of olive oil to the pan over medium heat and cook the sausage for about 10 minutes, until browned and cooked through.

8. Add the remaining 1 cup wine and the tomato paste, salt, and pepper to the sausage. Simmer for about 15 to 20 minutes, until the liquid has cooked off.

continued

for the filling

2 large leeks, white part only
(green tops removed)

¼ cup olive oil

2 cups white wine

1 cup chicken or vegetable stock

1 tablespoon packed
light brown sugar

2 pounds mild Italian sausage,
removed from casings

3 tablespoons tomato paste

1 teaspoon sea salt

Several grinds of black pepper

1 pound ricotta cheese,
drained if particularly watery

½ cup chopped fresh basil

6 pizza dough balls (homemade
or store-bought; whole wheat,
white, or a combination), at
room temperature

24 ounces fresh mozzarella,
cut into 1-ounce portions

9. Remove the sausage from the pan, and drain off the excess fat in a colander or sieve. Set aside or discard the fat (I feed mine to my dogs!).

10. Transfer the sausage to a medium bowl. Stir in the ricotta, basil, and prepared leeks. Set aside.

11. *Assemble the Calzones:* Preheat the oven to 400°F. Lightly oil two large, rimmed baking sheets.

12. On a lightly floured surface, cut each dough ball into 4 pieces and form into balls (for a total of 24 balls). This is most easily done with a metal dough cutter/scraper. Cover the dough balls with a kitchen cloth and leave to rest for 20 minutes.

13. Using floured hands and a floured surface, shape or push 12 balls of dough into 6-inch rounds.

14. Put 1 ounce of mozzarella onto one side of each dough round. Place about ½ cup of filling atop the mozzarella and spread over half of the round, leaving a ½-inch border. Moisten the entire circumference of the dough with wet fingers, fold the other half over the filling, and press the edges together to create a seal, using either your fingers or the tines of a fork.

15. Transfer the 12 calzones to the prepared baking sheets, 6 on each pan. Bake about 25 to 30 minutes, until nicely browned, rotating the position of the pans halfway through the cooking time.

16. Repeat the process with the remaining 12 dough balls, mozzarella, and filling.

17. Serve the calzones warm or at room temperature, with the dipping sauce. ⫷

»»» Chocolate Mint "Movie Stars"

Back before I became health conscious, **Junior Mints** *were my movie-time treat of choice. When I learned what was in them, though, I gave up the habit. Fortunately, making them from scratch involves simple ingredients and couldn't be easier to do. Cutting them into star shapes with a miniature cookie cutter gives a cheeky nod to the "stars" of the big screen.* **SERVINGS VARY, BASED ON SIZE OF COOKIE CUTTER USED**

YOU WILL NEED

2¼ cups powdered sugar, plus extra for rolling

2 tablespoons plus 2 teaspoons cold water

3 tablespoons coconut oil

1 tablespoon Lyle's Golden Syrup or light corn syrup

2 teaspoons peppermint extract

1½ cups dark chocolate chips or chunks

White nonpareils (I like to use the all-natural "Nature's Colors String of Pearls" made by India Tree)

TO MAKE

1. Line two rimmed baking sheets with wax paper and set aside.

2. Put the powdered sugar, cold water, 1 tablespoon of the coconut oil, the syrup, and the peppermint extract into a large bowl and combine with an electric mixer set on low-medium until the mixture begins to come together. Use a spatula to scrape down any powdered sugar clinging to the beaters or the bottom of the mixing bowl, as needed.

3. Lightly cover a countertop or work surface with powdered sugar and scrape the mint mixture out of the bowl onto the surface. You'll also want to coat your rolling pin and hands with a bit of powdered sugar to keep the filling from sticking as you roll it out.

4. Gently knead the filling until all the bits are fully incorporated and it feels smooth and elastic. Form into a flattened disk.

5. Using a rolling pin, roll the filling out to around ¼ inch thick. Cut shapes into the filling with a miniature star-shaped cookie cutter: press the cutter firmly into the filling, give it a gentle twist, and then place the star on one of the prepared baking sheets (you can place them rather close together). Continue cutting out shapes until all the filling has been used, rerolling scraps as necessary. All of the stars will fit on one baking sheet.

6. Place the baking sheets in the freezer for 25 minutes.

continued

7. About 10 minutes before removing the stars from the freezer, pour 2 inches of water into the bottom of a medium stockpot. Rest a large metal bowl on the rim of the pot to create a double boiler. Put the chocolate chips and remaining 2 tablespoons of coconut oil into the metal bowl and bring the water to a boil. Gently stir the chocolate until it has fully melted.

8. Remove the stars from the freezer. Using a long-tined fork, drop them one at a time into the melted chocolate, turning each star over twice so that it is fully covered with chocolate.

9. Using the fork, lift the stars out of the chocolate, allowing a good bit of it to drip off. Sprinkle nonpareils evenly over the stars to cover and transfer to the second prepared baking sheet. Continue until all the stars have been covered with chocolate.

10. Set the stars aside until the chocolate has fully firmed up. This can be anywhere from 2 to 3 hours, depending on the temperature of your home. If you're making these in a house whose indoor temperature exceeds 72°F, place them in the refrigerator to firm up.

11. Once the chocolate has set up, remove the stars from the paper, using a paring knife to cut away any extra "overflow" chocolate clinging to the shape. Alternatively, keep all the chocolate on there and serve—just chalk up the candies' rustic charm to the beauty of the handmade!

12. Store at room temperature in a lidded container for up to 1 week. I also highly recommend freezing or refrigerating these and eating them cold. ⋘

fall AND winter

»»» *falling leaves* «««
PICNIC

There is a single gingko tree growing on the small mountain knob on which my home is sited. It was planted long ago by the property's former owners, along with a magnolia, a river birch, several maples, and a handful of other specimen trees. Over twenty feet tall, the gingko reaches skyward, clad in delicate fan-shaped leaves that turn a vibrant, canary yellow each autumn. It is this particular tree more than any of the others on our property that always stirs in me a feeling of great seasonal anticipation. Unlike the maple that takes its time, turning from green to yellow to brown, its leaves gently wafting down over the course of weeks, the gingko casts off its foliage in one fast exhalation. Whether prompted by the first freeze or a mighty wind, the gingko moves from covered to barren within one day.

A Falling Leaves Picnic invites you to slow down, to quite literally come to your senses, to lean and loaf and take in the profound beauty that autumn provides. The splendor of this season truly embodies the very definition of ephemeral. Some trees transition languidly, holding tightly to their leaves, and others, like my gingko, rid their branches of baggage with a true sense of urgency. We seldom give ourselves the permission to do nothing but take in the view. For this picnic, however, that's just the thing you most want to do. Find a lovely grove of trees, get comfortable, and watch the magic, and message, of autumn as it moves to transform, release, and fall away.

✳ *to* MAKE & DO

SELECT A SITE

Since this picnic is all about viewing tree leaves, you'll clearly want to choose a site where deciduous trees are present. Whether that's a solidary maple in a public park or a grove of tulip poplars in a forested cove is entirely up to you. The photos for this picnic were taken at a pond in Montreat, North Carolina. It is in a wildlife sanctuary and lies adjacent to the Greybeard Trailhead parking area. I have frequented the pond numerous times over the years, by myself when I lived in Montreat as a teenager and with friends, with family, and with my husband and son. It is beautiful year-round, but come autumn, it is down-right bewitching.

LEAF ETCHINGS

Long after a glorious, freshly fallen leaf has lost its luster and crumbled into memory, leaf etchings will remain. Gather a leaf or collection of leaves that are not too brittle and have pronounced "spines" or veins running through them. Place them on a hard, flat surface with their veins facing upward. Cover with a sheet of plain white paper.

Unwrap a crayon in a color of your choosing. (You can mimic the leaf's current color or choose a shocking, vibrant hue—whatever you prefer.) Place the crayon on its side, and holding down the paper with your non-writing hand, rub the crayon back and forth across the paper until the image of leaf beneath emerges.

TIC-TAC-TOE

Where there are trees, there's bound to be twigs and acorns and pinecones. What are these arbor accoutrements if not the makings of a Tic-Tac-Toe board! Place sticks horizontally and vertically to create the game's frame, and then divvy up acorns and pinecones (or rocks and moss or berries and any other natural object) for each player. Ready, set, game on!

✳ *to* BEHOLD & EXPLORE

LEAF IDENTIFICATION

Bring along a tree and leaf identification guide specific to your geographic region. Gather leaves en route to your picnicking area, as well as from trees at your destination. Use the guide to correctly identify the leaves, and then gently place them inside the book's pages. The pressed leaves can later be framed as specimens or simply kept as mementos of the day.

to SAVOR & SIP

⟫ Ham, Gouda, *and* Pear Grilled Sandwiches

While grilled cheese sandwiches might not be the first foods to naturally come to mind for picnicking, the truth is they travel surprisingly well. Wrap up the hot sandwiches in parchment, wax paper, or in kitchen cloths for easy transport. Crisp apples can also be swapped in for pears, or added in addition. **MAKES 2 SANDWICHES**

YOU WILL NEED

2 tablespoons mayonnaise

1 tablespoon Dijon mustard

4 slices of a bread of your choosing (I used multigrain)

½ pound thinly sliced baked ham

½ pound smoked Gouda cheese

1 red pear, sliced thin

2 tablespoons salted butter, softened

TO MAKE

1. Begin by making an aioli: whisk together the mayonnaise and mustard in a small mixing bowl.

2. Arrange the bread slices on a cutting board. Divide the aioli among the slices and spread evenly.

3. Distribute the ham, Gouda, and pear evenly over 2 slices of the bread. Top each mound with the remaining 2 slices of bread, aioli side down, forming a sandwich. Butter the top of each sandwich with ½ tablespoon of butter.

4. Warm a heavy-bottomed saucepan or cast iron skillet over medium heat. Place the sandwiches in the pan, butter side down. Spread the remaining butter evenly over the top halves.

5. Cook until golden brown on the bottom, then flip and cook on the reverse side. When the cheese has melted, remove the sandwiches from the pan and transfer to a plate to cool. Cut in half and serve.

Note: These sandwiches can also be assembled in the same manner and cooked on a panini press. ⟪

»» Roasted Root Veggie Chips

When I discovered how easy these chips are to make and how flavorful they are, and how readily my young son will eat them without coaxing or coercion, I knew I'd found chip bliss. Any cooking spray will work, but I found the flavor and crispness of the chips to be enhanced by coconut oil. **MAKES 2 TO 3 CUPS**

YOU WILL NEED

1 medium beet (any color)

1 medium carrot

1 sweet potato

1 taro root, parsnip, or celeriac root

Coconut or olive oil cooking spray

Sea salt

TO MAKE

1. Preheat the oven to 275°F. Trim and peel the vegetables and set aside scraps for composting. Using a mandoline, slice the vegetables as thin as possible, anywhere from ⅛ to ¹⁄₁₆ inch thick is ideal.

2. Lightly spray two rimmed baking sheets with oil. Place the sliced vegetables in a single layer on the sheets. Give a second light spray of oil over the vegetables.

3. Place the baking sheets in the oven and bake for 1 hour, flipping the vegetable slices over halfway through the cooking time.

4. Remove the pans from the oven. Transfer the chips to a large bowl. Sprinkle with the salt and toss gently using clean hands. Allow the chips to cool completely before storing, then store in a lidded container at room temperature and consume within 1 week. «««

⟫ Grape Juice Spritz

One of my fondest indicators that autumn has truly arrived is the appearance of Concord grapes. Those indigo-hued orbs are packed with flavor, far more so than their green and light red kin. I suggest purchasing several pounds when you come across them, and freeze or can the juice for later use. **SERVES 4**

YOU WILL NEED

1 pound Concord grapes

1 tablespoon honey

¼ cup boiling water

Zest of 1 lemon

Ice cubes

Sparkling water

TO MAKE

1. Rinse the grapes under cold water. Remove them from their stems and place in a medium saucepan. Set the stems aside to compost. Press on the grapes with the back of a metal spoon or potato masher to release as much juice as possible.

2. Put the saucepan over medium heat. Continue pressing on the grapes until the mixture comes to a boil. Boil rapidly for 5 minutes. Remove from the heat and set aside to cool for 10 minutes.

3. Using a fine-mesh sieve placed atop a medium bowl, strain the juice. Compost the solids. Set the juice aside until cooled to room temperature.

4. Meanwhile, place the honey in a small bowl. Pour the boiling water over it and whisk to fully incorporate. Whisk in the lemon zest and set aside to cool.

5. To serve the spritzers, place about 3 or 4 ice cubes into 4 tumblers. Add 1 tablespoon of the honey and lemon syrup and ¼ cup of grape juice to each glass. Top off with sparkling water and stir gently to combine. ⟪

≫ PB&J Thumbprint Cookies

From kids to seniors, everyone knows that peanut butter and jelly were simply meant to go together. I took that notion and translated it into cookie form. A sprinkling of coarse flake salt adds a bit of sophistication to an otherwise youthful treat! **MAKES 3 DOZEN**

YOU WILL NEED

1½ cups all-purpose flour

¾ teaspoon baking soda

¾ teaspoon sea salt

½ cup (1 stick) salted butter, at room temperature

⅔ cup packed light brown sugar

⅓ cup granulated sugar

1 egg

1 teaspoon vanilla extract

1 cup peanut butter (smooth or chunky, depending on preference)

⅓ cup grape jelly

Coarse flake salt, such as Maldon

TO MAKE

1. Sift together the flour, baking soda, and salt. Set aside. Line two rimmed baking sheets with parchment paper or silicone baking mats.

2. In a medium bowl, beat the butter, brown sugar, and granulated sugar using an electric mixer until well creamed. Scrape down the beaters with a spatula. Add the egg and vanilla extract and beat until light and fluffy, 2 to 3 minutes. Scrape down the beaters and bowl again, and then beat in the peanut butter until fully incorporated.

3. Add half of the flour mixture and beat at low speed until incorporated. Scrape down the beaters and bowl. Repeat with the rest of the flour mixture. Place the dough in the refrigerator to chill for 20 minutes.

4. Preheat the oven to 375°F. Roll the dough into tablespoon-size balls. Space evenly on the prepared baking sheets, 12 cookies on each sheet. Using your thumb, make an indentation into the center of each cookie. Place enough jelly into each indentation to fill it.

5. Bake for 15 minutes, rotating the baking sheets halfway through the baking time. Remove from the oven and sprinkle with the salt. Allow the cookies to cool on the baking sheets for 5 minutes, then transfer to a cooling rack to cool completely. Repeat the process with the remaining cookie dough.

6. Store in a lidded container and consume within 3 or 4 days. ≪

» high-altitude «

PICNIC

The most amazing thing happens when you reach the top of a mountain. No matter how high the elevation, and pretty much regardless of the setting, when a summit is reached, the same experience occurs. Whether atop the jagged peaks of the Rockies or the soft, undulating crests of the Blue Ridge Mountains, life gets very quiet at higher altitudes. The air is less dense, and there are fewer things around to make or reflect noise. As a result, everything is more still, more muted, more hushed when you climb to the upper reaches, making a high-altitude picnic an ideal setting for taking in the views, satisfying the palate, and enjoying the silence.

Black Balsam Knob is found in the Pisgah National Forest near milepost 420 on the Blue Ridge Parkway. It is the twenty-third-highest of the forty mountains in North Carolina over 6,000 feet.

The top of the Black Balsam is a grassy mountain bald offering panoramic views. To say it is stunning is to call water wet. It is majestic and resplendent and magnificent and pretty much every superlative that can be employed for describing awe-inspiring settings. It is my most beloved place to hike in my area, which is why I have traveled there for my birthday each year for the past several years. It is also the setting for this picnic.

A picnic atop a mountain might sound like a whole lot of fun but also a whole lot of work. With a bit of planning and preparation, though, it will be highly memorable, for all the right reasons! You'll be climbing upward, which means you'll be using the strength of your entire body to get there. Owing to that, you'll want to carry dinnerware that is as lightweight as possible and easy-to-carry foods that keep well without a cooler.

I recommend using aluminum ware or enamelware for serving plates and food storage containers. Both aren't heavy and can take any knocking around they may encounter during the hike and picnic in a rocky, mountain setting. A sturdy backpack is ideal for carrying your picnic goods, a pair of quality hiking boots a great idea for helping you find your footing safely, and a can-do attitude is essential for making the day as epic as the views!

SELECT A SITE

When considering locations for this picnic, you'll need to adjust your altitude, as it were. High elevations are what's called for, so put on your hiking boots, strap on a backpack, and head onward and upward. While it needn't be Mt. Everest, a gentle knoll at the local park isn't exactly ideal, either. Somewhere in the middle will make for the most comfortable High-Altitude Picnic spot.

USE A COMPASS

There is quite possibly no better time to pull out a compass than when on a hike up a mountain. Although most trails will be clearly marked (and it's best to stay on them to avoid harming fragile habitats and ecosystems nearby), understanding navigation can be highly worthwhile when exploring the great outdoors. Once you've reached your summit, use a compass to find out which direction you're facing, and then orient yourself to your surroundings from there. Also, in the event that you should get lost while out adventuring, a compass is exactly the tool you want to have on hand.

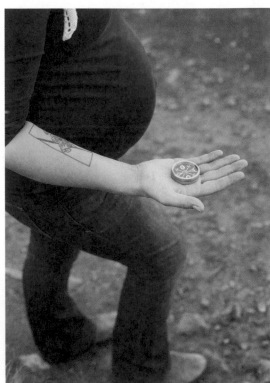

✳ *to* BEHOLD & EXPLORE

SIGNS OF WILDLIFE

As you hike to your destination, become an amateur tracker. Look for signs of the presence of wildlife. From paw prints to scratch marks on trees to droppings, silent calling cards are being left by the wild creatures inhabiting your picnic spot. Bird nests, beaver dams, toad holes, and so much more give testament to the wildness around you. Be prepared to actually come across a wild creature. Keep your eyes down for snakes and your voice audible, to deter bears. Whether firsthand or indirect, encounters with wildlife can be absolutely exhilarating!

IDENTIFY MOUNTAIN RANGES

I live in the Blue Ridge Mountains, where hikes to mountaintops are part of my regular routine. I especially enjoy observing and identifying distant mountain ranges once I've reached a summit or other high vantage point. Bring along a trail guide specific to your region. Use your compass to determine your direction and then turn to your guide to help you distinguish all the features of the land within view.

✶ to SAVOR & SIP ✶

››› Beef Jerky

Beef jerky is a quintessential hiking food. Highly transportable and dense with nutrients, it's completely understandable why a bit of jerky is just as essential for some hikers as a sturdy pair of boots and a water bottle. Purchasing high-quality jerky, though, can be a bit costly, which is why this recipe is so great. Flank steak is affordable and readily accessible at most butchers and meat counters. Once prepared, this jerky will keep for a couple of weeks or so in the refrigerator, making the time involved in it completely worthwhile. **SERVES 6 TO 8**

YOU WILL NEED

1½ pounds grass-fed flank steak

¼ cup honey

2 ounces rye whiskey

2 tablespoons Worcestershire sauce

2 tablespoons malt vinegar

1 tablespoon soy sauce

1 tablespoon prepared brown mustard

1 tablespoon chipotle hot sauce

1 tablespoon sea salt

2 teaspoons granulated garlic

Several grinds of black pepper

TO MAKE

1. Trim the fat off of the flank steak, then cut it across the grain into thin strips about ⅛ inch thick.

2. Combine the honey, whiskey, Worcestershire sauce, vinegar, soy sauce, mustard, hot sauce, salt, and garlic in a mixing bowl. Pour the marinade into a baking pan and add the meat strips. Stir to coat the meat, then cover and refrigerate for at least 3 hours or overnight.

3. Preheat the oven to 170°F. Place a wire cooling rack on a rimmed baking sheet. Remove the meat strips from the marinade and place them on the wire rack.

4. Put the baking sheet into the oven and heat for 3 hours.

5. Flip the strips over and grind black pepper over them.

6. Heat for another hour, check for doneness, then continue to check every half hour until done, up to about 6½ hours. Cooking time will depend on the thickness of the strips and water content of the meat. The jerky is done when it breaks gently when bent but is not brittle. It should not snap (that means you went too far).

7. Let it cool completely on the wire rack, then transfer to a jar and keep in the refrigerator for up to 2 weeks. Let it return to room temperature before eating. ‹‹‹

» Roasted Carrot *and* Fennel Dip

Trail bars are another indispensible hiking food. Many feature carrots and nuts in some incarnation, so this is my play on the iconic treat. Instead of a bar, I'm offering a dip. No dairy in the recipe means it can go without refrigeration for many hours, similar to hummus. **MAKES ABOUT 3 CUPS**

YOU WILL NEED

for the dip

1½ pounds carrots

1½ pounds fennel (fronds reserved)

¾ cup plus 1 tablespoon olive oil

1 cup pecans

3 garlic cloves, peeled

1 tablespoon balsamic vinegar

2 teaspoons sea salt

Several grinds of black pepper

1 teaspoon ground coriander

¼ bunch of fresh cilantro or parsley

for the topping

½ cup dried fruit, such as raisins
   and apricots

2 tablespoons olive oil

1 cup of your favorite nuts,
   chopped

1 tablespoon honey

½ teaspoon sea salt

A few grinds of black pepper

Cucumber slices and/or crackers,
   to serve

TO MAKE

1. *Prepare the Dip:* Preheat the oven to 450°F.

2. Trim and peel the carrots and cut down the middle lengthwise. Trim the stems off the fennel and cut the bulbs in half.

3. Warm 1 tablespoon of the olive oil in a cast iron skillet over medium heat. Add the pecans, stir to coat, and toast until fragrant, 2 to 3 minutes. Set aside to cool.

4. On a rimmed baking sheet, toss the carrots, fennel, and garlic cloves with ¼ cup of the olive oil. Roast in the oven for about 45 minutes, until the edges have begun to brown.

5. Remove the baking sheet from the oven. Let the vegetables sit for a few minutes until cool enough to handle, then chop into small pieces.

6. Put the vegetables into a food processor (or a medium bowl if using a handheld immersion blender). Add the toasted pecans, balsamic vinegar, the remaining ½ cup olive oil, salt, pepper, and coriander. Blend until smooth, scraping down the sides with a spatula as necessary.

7. Add the cilantro and reserved fennel fronds, and blend some more, until the green flecks are evenly distributed. Transfer the dip to a lightweight travel container with a tight-fitting lid.

8. *Prepare the Topping:* Cut any large pieces of dried fruit into pieces the size of a large raisin or so.

9. Heat the olive oil in a small skillet, over medium heat. Add the nuts, fruit, honey, salt, and pepper. Cook, stirring frequently, until the mixture is fragrant and just starting to brown, about 2 minutes.

10. Allow to cool slightly, then top the dip with it.

11. Serve the dip with cucumber slices and crackers. «

»» Trail Mix Blondies

A playful nod to trail mix is my final take on classic hiking edibles. I've nestled granola and choco-late chips into a blondie bar, creating a highly transportable food that can be eaten with your hands, no need for utensils. Do be sure to select a somewhat fatty granola, such as Dried Cherry Granola (page 25). **SERVES 9 TO 12**

YOU WILL NEED

½ cup (1 stick) unsalted butter, melted

¾ cup packed light brown sugar

¼ cup granulated sugar

1 large egg

2 teaspoons vanilla extract

1 cup all-purpose flour

1 teaspoon sea salt

½ cup chocolate chips

1 cup granola

TO MAKE

1. Preheat the oven to 350°F. Butter an 8 × 8-inch baking pan and set aside.

2. In a medium bowl, beat together the melted butter, brown sugar, and granulated sugar with an electric mixer until smooth and fluffy, about 3 to 4 minutes. Scrape down the beaters with a spatula.

3. Add the egg and vanilla and beat until well incorporated. Scrape down the beaters again.

4. Add the flour and salt, beating until just incorporated. Stir in the chocolate chips and granola.

5. Transfer the mixture to the prepared pan and spread out evenly using a spatula. Bake for 25 to 30 minutes, until the top is golden and a knife inserted into the center comes out clean.

6. Allow to cool for 15 minutes before serving. «««

» coffee break «

PICNIC

*B*ack *when I worked an eight-hour workday,* before I traded in a stable paycheck for the comfort of working at home in my pajamas, I used to really love my paid breaks. In the United States, federal regulations permit those working eight-hour days to have a paid half-hour lunch break as well as two 15-minute breaks during their shift. When your job isn't quite your passion—even if you appreciate its ability to aid you in obtaining food and shelter nonetheless—there's a good deal of workday clock-watching involved. I learned to really, really crave those bits of time that carved up the day and permitted me a moment, however fleeting, to return to myself, and come away renewed and invigorated.

Whether you work from home as I now do or clock in elsewhere for the day, a coffee break, I've come to believe, is a wonderful way of recharging. It needn't be long, but it should be deliberate. Above all else, it absolutely should be delicious. We are sensory beings, and breaking up long stretches of time can be significantly expedited by fully engaging our senses. A Coffee Break Picnic provides the opportunity to take in a new setting visually, enables you to move and stimulate your body and breath, ignites your taste buds, and enlivens your olfactory system. Fragrant, aromatic, beautiful, and tactile—let this be your coffee break mantra. It won't change your job, but it'll change your attitude, guaranteed.

SELECT A SITE

Coffee is a stimulant. When you drink it, it's typically because you want a little extra pep, some supplemental zip and energy. Accordingly, when selecting a site for a Coffee Break Picnic, consider somewhere that is itself stimulating. A bustling city park, a room with a captivating view, a vibrant building foyer—anywhere that's got a good deal of activity and buzz would be fitting.

DEEP BREATHING

A coffee break is, by nature, brief. Many of us will only have about 15 or so minutes to regroup before getting back to whatever task is at hand. Taking some deep breaths during this time, coupled with the invigorating nature of coffee, will go far toward putting some pep back into your step.

STRETCHES

After you've taken some sips of coffee and inhaled its invigorating aroma, take a moment to stretch. Arm, leg, or back stretches, or, even better, a combination of all three will oxygenate your muscles and help alleviate fatigue.

FOREIGN NUMBERS

Seize the opportunity to learn numbers in a foreign language. Create flash cards out of cardstock or index cards. Within several coffee breaks, you can teach yourself to count to ten in a variety of languages!

	FRENCH	SPANISH	ITALIAN
1	Un	Uno	Uno
2	Deux	Dos	Due
3	Trois	Tres	Tre
4	Quatre	Cuatro	Quattro
5	Cinq	Cinco	Cinque
6	Six	Seis	Sei
7	Sept	Siete	Sette
8	Huit	Ocho	Otto
9	Neuf	Nueve	Nove
10	Dix	Diez	Dieci

FOREIGN WORDS

Similarly, explore your environment through the lens of a foreign language. For example, if it's a parklike atmosphere you take your coffee break in, select words in another language that relate to that setting. This can be especially helpful if you have plans, or aspirations, to travel to a particular country in the near future.

to savor & sip

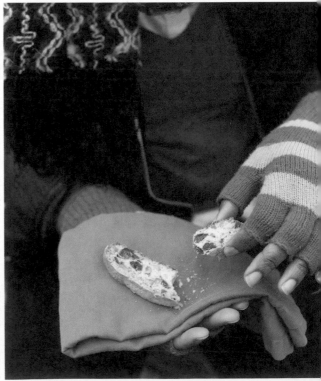

»» Pistachio, Apricot, *and* Fennel Biscotti

I have been baking and enjoying biscotti for over twenty years, playing with all manner of flavor pairings along the way. The combination of pistachios, dried apricots, and fennel seeds offered here might just be my favorite yet. With a bit of crunch from the nuts, sweetness and chewiness from the fruit, and the aroma of the fennel, there's something here to please every palate. **MAKES 2 DOZEN**

YOU WILL NEED

2 cups all-purpose flour

1 teaspoon baking powder

Pinch of sea salt

4 tablespoons (½ stick) unsalted butter, at room temperature

1 cup sugar

3 eggs

1 teaspoon vanilla extract

1 cup roasted pistachios, coarsely chopped

½ cup dried apricots, chopped

2 teaspoons fennel seeds

TO MAKE

1. Preheat the oven to 350°F. Line two baking sheets with parchment paper or silicone baking mats and set aside.

2. In a medium bowl, combine the flour, baking powder, and salt. Set aside. In another medium bowl, beat together the butter and sugar with an electric mixer until pale and fluffy, about 2 to 3 minutes. Scrape down the sides of the bowl and the beaters with a spatula as necessary. Add the eggs, one at a time, beating after each addition and then scraping down the bowl. Beat in the vanilla.

3. Add the flour mixture. Beat just until everything is fully combined, about 20 to 30 seconds. Add the pistachios, apricots, and fennel seeds, and beat just until they are fully incorporated into the dough.

4. Divide the dough in half. Place each half on a prepared baking sheet. Shape each piece of dough into a 3 × 8-inch log. Bake for 30 to 35 minutes, just until the tops begin to crack and turn golden brown.

5. Remove the baking sheets from the oven. Allow the logs to cool in the pan for 30 minutes. Transfer them to a cutting board and, using a serrated knife, cut on a diagonal into ½-inch-thick slices.

6. Place the slices, cut side down, on the baking sheets. Return to the oven and bake an additional 15 to 20 minutes, until golden brown, flipping the slices over about halfway through the baking time. Remove the baking sheets from the oven. Allow the biscotti to cool in the pan for about 5 minutes, then transfer to cooling racks to cool completely. Store in an airtight, lidded container and consume within 3 to 5 days. «««

⫸ Flavored Coffee

Ever since becoming a mother in 2010, I begin my mornings with a cup of coffee. I just need that extra zip to get me going. Not wanting to ingest the fixatives, stabilizers, and additives included in store-bought flavored coffees but unwilling to forgo flavorful options, I decided instead to create my own. Doing so is both spectacularly easy and imminently delicious. **MAKES 4 CUPS**

YOU WILL NEED

Coffee beans (enough for a
  4-cup pot of coffee)

Water

flavoring options (choose one)

Cardamom seeds, taken from
  2 green pods

1 whole clove

½ of a 2-inch cinnamon stick or
  1 teaspoon ground cinnamon

½ star anise pod

½ teaspoon freshly grated nutmeg

Vanilla bean seeds, scraped from
  ¼ vanilla bean pod

TO MAKE

1. Place enough coffee beans for a four-cup pot of coffee and the spice of your choosing into a coffee grinder. Grind to your desired texture.

2. Brew the coffee using a French press, Moka pot, or drip coffeemaker according to the manufacturer's instructions.

3. If not using right away, store the ground blend in a metal canister, glass jar, or brown coffee bag. Although best if used upon grinding, the blend will stay fresh for up to 1 week at room temperature or 3 or 4 weeks in the freezer. ⫷

⟫⟫ Orangettes

Strips of candied orange peel enrobed in chocolate, orangettes are wildly flavorful. They're also practically perfect for enjoying with coffee, making them an ideal addition to this picnic. **MAKES 3 TO 4 DOZEN**

YOU WILL NEED

2 oranges

1½ cups sugar

1 cup water

1 cup chopped baking chocolate (60% cocoa content or higher)

½ cup roasted almonds, pistachios, or hazelnuts, finely chopped (optional)

TO MAKE

1. Place a wire cooling rack on a rimmed baking sheet. Line another baking sheet with parchment paper or a silicone baking mat and set aside.

2. Cut off the top and bottom of each orange. Make 4 scoring indentations around the remaining peel, from top to bottom. Pull off the peels and scrape out any pith from the inside with a spoon. Cut the sections into ¼-inch strips.

3. Bring a small saucepan filled with several inches of cold tap water to a boil. Add the strips and boil for 1 minute. Drain the peels in a colander and then rinse under cold water. Repeat this process with fresh water two more times.

4. Return the empty saucepan to the stove. Add the sugar and 1 cup of water and heat over medium-high heat. Stir until the sugar dissolves. Turn the heat to high and bring the mixture to a boil. Add the orange strips. Reduce the heat to low and simmer, uncovered, until soft and translucent, about 25 to 30 minutes.

5. Using tongs, remove the peels from the saucepan. Place the peels on the wire rack on the baking sheet. Leave to dry for at least 4 hours, or until the sugar has firmed up on them and they're not terribly sticky to the touch.

6. Once the peels are dry, melt the chocolate in a double boiler or microwave. Dip each strip into the melted chocolate about three-quarters of the way in, shake off any excess drips, and place onto the wax paper or silicone baking mat. As you go, sprinkle the chopped nuts over the chocolate before it hardens. Set side to cool. Store in an airtight lidded container and use within 1 week. ⟪⟪

»»» tailgate «««

PICNIC

For some people, myself included, the excitement surrounding the shift from summer to autumn is all about the leaves. When the forests surrounding my house begin to shed acorns and gently drop their foliage, shifting from emerald to ocher, rust, ruby, and sienna, I know good times are in store. For others, though, the draw away from Popsicles and beach trips, toward sweaters and hot cider, is all about game day.

I grew up with a father who was deeply in love with football. From collegiate weekend games to Monday-night big-league showdowns, if there was a game to be witnessed, he was watching it. I can immediately conjure up images of him pumping the air with his fist, Arsenio Hall–style, when his preferred team ran a touchdown. During our every-other-weekend drives between his house and my mom's, in the days before smart devices and in-car television systems, we'd pass the time reciting the names of the teams of the NFL.

Although I'm not the sports fan he was (and continues to be), I completely appreciate his devotion to the game. We all crave camaraderie and companionship, something to unify and endear us to one another. Sports can do that for people. You needn't know anything else about a person other than that they're a fan of the same team you're a fan of, and you have common ground. It's an immediate connector, requiring little else than mutual fandom.

My father's alma mater is Notre Dame, which is also that of his twin brothers, Pete and Lloyd, my brother Walker, my sister Theo, and my cousins Lloyd Jr., Ed, Patrick, and Laura. Accordingly, football season is a big deal in my family. Many of them still travel to South Bend, Indiana, and engage in a bit of parking lot tailgating before the big game, with abundant food and drink.

I'm tailgating too, come autumn, but I'm typically doing it up on the Blue Ridge Parkway, at a scenic overlook, or down some beautiful country road, quite literally eating at the tailgate of our car. Wherever you find yourself come tailgating season, the recipes here are sure to fill your appetite. At the big game or leaf peeping, this autumn I invite you to pack a basket, grab some blankets, put on your warmest sweater, and experience the thrill of a Tailgate Picnic!

✳ to MAKE & DO

SELECT A SITE

What defines an "ideal" Tailgate Picnic site is entirely up to your interests. If sports are your thing, then a parking lot picnic is the way to go. If scenic vistas are your passion, then seek out a quiet country road, national or historic byway, or glorious roadside overlook.

LEAF GRADIENTS

Tailgating season is also leaf season. An assortment of colors will be on display, both over-head and underfoot. Color gradients are sequences of hues (color) and values (darkness), moving across the light spectrum (remember ROYGBIV—red, orange, yellow, green, blue, indigo, violet?). Gather up some leaves and fashion a leaf gradient at your site. It's lovely to look at, and a silent homage to the stunning colors of the season.

TOSS A BALL

Whether you elect to tailgate in the great outdoors taking in a scenic view or in a parking lot waiting for the big game to start, consider getting a little physical yourself. Bring along a football or soccer ball and work up an appetite running around!

✳ to BEHOLD & EXPLORE

GROW TREES

Oak trees drop acorns in abundance come autumn. At your tailgating site, see if you can find a few to gather. Once home, pot the acorns in soil and attempt to grow seedlings. Once they're large enough, plant the trees either in your yard or, if permitted, back at your picnicking location, to serve as a living memento of the day.

AUTUMN EQUINOX

Consider having this picnic on the autumnal equinox in late September. On that day, the sun will rise exactly due east and set precisely due west, just one of two times a year for such an occurrence. It's also typically a time of year riddled with crisp, cool days, ideal for taking a scenic drive or enjoying a football game, whatever your preference dictates.

⋙ Twice-Baked Potatoes

To me, fewer foods say "comfort" like stuffed potatoes. Crunchy and earthy on the outside yet smooth and fluffy inside, these potatoes are perfect tailgating fare. Top them with Cheesy Roasted Broccoli (page 184) and All-Beef Chili (page 185) for a hearty, warming meal. **SERVES 12**

YOU WILL NEED

12 medium baking potatoes

2 tablespoons olive oil

¾ cup sour cream

¾ cup (1½ sticks) salted butter, at room temperature

2 eggs, beaten

1 teaspoon sea salt

Several grinds of black pepper

2 tablespoons chopped fresh chives

About ½ ounce Parmesan cheese, for grating

TO MAKE

1. Preheat the oven to 400°F.

2. Poke the potatoes a couple times with a fork. Place on a large, rimmed baking sheet. Pour the olive oil over them and then toss to fully coat. Place the pan in the oven and roast for 1 hour.

3. Remove from the oven and let sit for a few minutes. Cut the potatoes in half lengthwise. Carefully scoop out most of the insides into a medium bowl, leaving a thin layer of potato on the inside of the skins. Return the skins to the baking sheet.

4. Add the sour cream, butter, eggs, salt, pepper, and chives to the potato flesh. Stir until fully incorporated.

5. Spoon the mixture back into the potato skins, dividing it evenly until all are filled.

6. Grate a little Parmesan over the tops of the potatoes. Roast in the oven for 30 minutes. Remove from the oven and allow to cool slightly before serving.

Note: You can scale up or scale down the number of potatoes based on the amount of people you'll be feeding. For every potato, 1 tablespoon of butter and 1 tablespoon of sour cream should be used. ⋘

»» Cheesy Roasted Broccoli

Most otherwise perfectly acceptable cheesy broccoli dishes are done in by steamed or boiled broccoli. The results are either tough and watery or flaccid and flavorless, neither of which will taste any better when doused in a cheese sauce. My trick is to first roast the broccoli. This eliminates excess moisture while concentrating flavor, providing delicious bits of caramelized, crisp broccoli spears. Top that with cheese sauce, and you'll make a broccoli fan out of anyone. **SERVES 8 TO 10**

YOU WILL NEED

2 large broccoli crowns, chopped into bite-size pieces

¼ cup olive oil

1 teaspoon sea salt

Several grinds of black pepper

4 tablespoons (½ stick) salted butter, at room temperature

½ cup all-purpose flour

1 cup heavy cream

1 tablespoon Worcestershire sauce

8 ounces shredded cheddar cheese

TO MAKE

1. Preheat the oven to 400°F.

2. Place the broccoli pieces on a large, rimmed baking sheet. Drizzle the olive oil over the broccoli. Sprinkle with the salt and pepper and then toss to fully coat. Roast for about 40 minutes, until slightly browned.

3. In a medium saucepan, beat the butter and flour together with a spoon to make a smooth paste.

4. Over medium-low heat, melt the butter and flour paste, stirring constantly until it starts to bubble. Slowly stir in the cream. Add the Worcestershire sauce and cheese, stirring until fully melted and all ingredients are incorporated, then turn off the heat.

5. Stir in the roasted broccoli, and keep warm until ready to serve. ⫷

⋙ All-Beef Chili

For me, the aroma of a pot of chili cooking is one of the greatest scents a kitchen is capable of producing. Smoky, herbaceous, and earthy all at once, chili is just plain delicious. Dollop liberally onto the Twice-Baked Potatoes (page 183), if you're so inclined. **SERVES 8 TO 10**

YOU WILL NEED

2 tablespoons olive oil, plus more if necessary

2 pounds lean, grass-fed ground beef

1 large onion, diced

1 large red bell pepper, diced

4 garlic cloves, minced

One 28-ounce can fire-roasted diced tomatoes

1 cup beef stock

¼ cup tomato paste

1 tablespoon sea salt

1 tablespoon dried oregano

1 tablespoon smoky paprika

1 tablespoon cocoa powder

1 tablespoon ground cumin

1 teaspoon chipotle powder

Hot sauce (optional)

TO MAKE

1. Heat 2 tablespoons olive oil in a medium saucepan over medium-high heat. Add the ground beef and cook until browned, about 15 minutes.

2. Remove the beef from the pot, leaving any grease behind. If the pan is dry, add a couple more tablespoons of olive oil. However, if more than 2 tablespoons of grease are left in the pan, drain the excess off. Either way, you want to end up with around 2 tablespoons of oil or fat in the pan.

3. Add the onion and bell pepper to the saucepan over medium-high heat. Sauté until they start to brown, about 10 minutes.

4. Add the garlic. Cook, stirring constantly, for 2 minutes, then add the browned beef and the tomatoes, stock, tomato paste, sea salt, oregano, paprika, cocoa, cumin, and chipotle powder. Reduce the heat to low.

5. Simmer for about 1 hour, adding a little extra beef stock if necessary (don't let the pan get dry).

6. Keep warm until ready to serve. Serve with hot sauce on the side for those who like a bit more heat.

Note: This is an all-beef chili, but if chili just isn't chili without beans for you, feel free to include them. Kidney or pinto beans would work equally well here. ⋘

»» Mason Jar Apple Cardamom Crumbles

Apple and cardamom are a divine pairing if there ever was one. The two simply bring out the best in each other. For picnicking portability, I thought it would be fun to both bake and serve the crumbles in small mason jars. Bake up the treats, cover with their lids, and dessert is deliciously ready to go!

MAKES 8 HALF-PINT JARS

YOU WILL NEED

for the crumble topping

¾ cup old-fashioned rolled oats

¾ cup all-purpose flour

¼ cup granulated sugar

¼ cup packed dark brown sugar

2 teaspoons ground cardamom

1 teaspoon sea salt

½ cup (1 stick) unsalted butter, at room temperature

for the filling

3 pounds apples (a mixture of varieties will yield the best flavor), peeled, cored, quartered, and cut into rough chunks

⅓ cup sugar

3 tablespoons all-purpose flour

¼ cup currants

Zest of 1 lemon

TO MAKE

1. Preheat the oven to 400°F. Place 8 half-pint mason jars on a rimmed baking sheet and set aside.

2. *Prepare the Crumble Topping:* Put the oats, flour, granulated sugar, brown sugar, cardamom, and salt in a medium bowl. Stir together until combined.

3. Using a pastry cutter or clean hands, cut the butter into the mixture until it is incorporated but some large chunks remain. Place in the refrigerator to chill while you prepare the filling.

4. *Prepare the Filling:* Put all the ingredients in a medium bowl. Using a mixing spoon or clean hands, toss together until all the apple pieces are coated.

5. *Assemble the Crumbles:* Divide the apple mixture evenly among the 8 mason jars. Top with the crumble topping. You may need to press the crumble down a bit into the filling in order to fit it all in.

6. Bake for 45 to 60 minutes, until the tops are golden brown. Let cool for at least 15 minutes before serving. These are especially good at room temperature. «««

» rooftop «

PICNIC

I live in a 1930s bungalow tucked into a mountain cove in western North Carolina. My surrounding environment is pretty much at eye level. Which is why city life can be equal parts thrilling and daunting to me: the sky-scrapers and high-rises all point to the abundance of life lived vertically, as opposed to at my horizontal orientation. Whenever I visit New York City or San Francisco or Chicago and pull back the curtains of my hotel room, I am floored—not so much by the view of the city itself but simply by the very act of being "above it all."

The first memory I have of being at a higher elevation is on the roof of my father's wife's apartment. At the time, she lived at Fox Hall, a beautiful apartment building in Washington, D.C. A former secretary of state had occupied the apartment previously. Her bathroom was huge and covered entirely in white marble, and there were an Olympic-size pool and sauna in the basement for residents to use anytime, twenty-four hours a day. The views from the roof, though, were her apartment's most riveting feature. I remember finding them simply intoxicating. The bell tower of the National Cathedral could be seen in the distance, as well as the Washington Monument's tall spire.

Later, in my mid-twenties, my father, his wife, and my siblings and I were vacationing in Rosemary Beach, Florida. Located on what is referred to as the state's "Panhandle," the beach is characterized by crystal clear, turquoise-hued waters for which that area is internationally known. One evening, after a meal at our rental home, Dad made reservations for drinks and dessert at a local restaurant specializing in Mediterranean cuisine. Our table was situated on the restaurant's rooftop terrace. As we nibbled on expertly crafted desserts and sipped coffee with Sambuca, the moon hung low, lighting up the kinetic waters, and I became overwhelmed, again, with the perspective afforded at a higher altitude.

A rooftop picnic is a fun way of enjoying life outdoors while still remaining close to the hum of activity. Accesses to roofs range from a simple walk up a flight of stairs to a ladder to a small entry port. Keep proper footwear, dress, and picnic packing in mind based on the particulars of your rooftop destination. Whatever the case, know that the change of view will be exhilarating, captivating, and inspiring!

✳ to MAKE & DO

SELECT A SITE

When considering a roof for picnicking on, look for one with a level surface. Pitched roofs are wonderful for rain runoff but not quite as dandy for laying out a blanket and picnicking upon. If you don't have access to a flat roof area of your own, ask friends or family members who live in apartment buildings. Wherever you end up, be certain to obtain permission in advance, as some buildings have prohibitions against roof use.

PORTABLE UTENSIL HOLDER

A utensil carrier is indispensable for keeping forks, spoons, and knives right where they need to be: within easy reach. This carrier includes a metal handle on top, perfect for toting it up to a rooftop or to any other picnicking spot.

✳ to BEHOLD & EXPLORE

SKYLINE SURVEY

I always love exploring new vantage points. My son is a toddler, and I'll often crouch down to meet his gaze and examine what life looks like when you're three feet tall. It is the same with increases in altitude. Taking in the world from a new height is fascinating, and filled with opportunities for playful discovery. Check out otherwise familiar landmarks from the rooftop. Is there anything that you've never noticed before, or perhaps that can be appreciated more fully from on high?

diy utensil holder

The beauty in making your own portable utensil carrier is in customizing its dimensions to fit your particular needs. Honestly, there aren't any hard-and-fast measurements for doing this right. So long as you have four sides, a bottom, dividers, and a handle, you're in good shape! Let your specific needs and your creativity serve as your guide.

YOU WILL NEED

One I × 6-inch wooden board, 4 feet long

One I × 4-inch wooden board, 6 feet long

I½-inch screws or finishing nails, for attaching the boards

½-inch screws, for attaching the handle

Metal outdoor door handle, large or small depending on project size

Paint

TO MAKE

1. Cut the wooden boards to your desired lengths, creating 4 sides, a bottom, and dividers. Using an electric drill and screws or a hammer and finishing nails, attach boards together to make whatever size utensil box you prefer. Screw the metal handle to the top, centering it in the middle of the carrier

2. Keep in mind what you ultimately intend to use the box for. It can also hold napkins, condiments, or other picnic items such as bug spray. Try not to make it bigger than you need. You want to be able to access the things that it holds as easily as possible but don't want it to be cumbersome to carry.

3. Paint or stain it to your liking. For a particularly nice distressed look, paint the box, let it dry, then paint it in a contrasting color. After it is completely dry, sand the box so that the edges of the first color show through.

to SAVOR & SIP

》》 Dijon Mustard Pork Chop Sandwich

For me, the hallmark of a particularly tasty meal is immediately wanting more of it after my portion has been consumed. Which is precisely what happens after I eat this sandwich. The pork chops are bathed in a mustard, honey, wine, and vinegar marinade for several hours, resulting in spectacularly tender, flavorful meat. Served with a mound of Mojito Slaw (page 195) on top, you'll likely be asking for "more, please" yourself! **SERVES 6 TO 8**

YOU WILL NEED

2 pounds thin-cut (¾ inch) boneless pork chops

Sea salt

1 cup white wine

¼ cup white wine vinegar

¼ cup Dijon mustard

¼ cup honey

Several grinds of black pepper

Olive oil

Loaf of sliced bread, to serve

Sweet pickle relish mixed with mayonnaise, to serve (optional)

Mojito Slaw (page 195)

TO MAKE

1. Lay the pork chops on a cutting board. Cover with a bit of wax or parchment paper. Using a meat pounder, pound the chops to about ½ inch thick. Place on a rimmed baking sheet large enough to accommodate all the pork chops. Sprinkle a bit of salt over the chops, then flip them and sprinkle the other side.

2. In a small saucepan over low heat, whisk together the white wine, vinegar, mustard, and honey. Once the marinade mixture is warm to the touch, remove from the heat. Pour the marinade over the pork chops, turning to coat on both sides.

3. Cover the baking sheet and place in the refrigerator. Leave to marinate for several hours or overnight, turning the pork chops at least once.

4. Remove the baking sheet from the refrigerator. Remove the pork chops from the marinade and place on a clean plate or small platter. Reserve the marinade.

5. Lightly sprinkle both sides of each chop with salt and a few grinds of black pepper.

6. Warm a skillet or medium saucepan over medium-high heat and add enough olive oil to coat the bottom of the pan. Working in batches, cook the pork chops until cooked through, about 4 minutes per side. Add oil as needed to coat the pan.

continued

7. Place the cooked chops on a clean cutting board. Let the meat rest for at least 10 minutes, then cut across the grain into thin, 1/8-inch slices.

8. Meanwhile, in a saucepan over medium-high heat, reduce the marinade until it starts to get a bit syrupy. Transfer to a medium bowl, add the pork slices, and toss to coat.

9. To serve, spread 2 slices of bread with a bit of sweet pickle relish mixed with mayonnaise, if desired. Place several pork slices on 1 prepared slice of bread, add a mound of Mojito Slaw, and top with the other slice. Repeat, making sandwiches until all the pork is used up. ⋘

⟫ Mojîto Slaw

With a nod to the mint and lime flavors associated with the mojito cocktail, this slaw offers an unrivaled bright, perky flavor, and it comes together in minutes. Do try to give it ample time for marinating, though, as the longer it sits, the better the flavors meld and amplify. **SERVES 6 TO 8**

YOU WILL NEED

1 green cabbage

Juice of 3 limes

2 tablespoons sugar

¼ cup olive oil

1 cup lightly packed mint leaves, chopped

2 teaspoons sea salt

Several grinds of black pepper

TO MAKE

1. Using a mandoline, food processor, or large kitchen knife, shred the cabbage. Put into a large bowl.

2. In a small saucepan over medium-low heat, gently warm the lime juice. Add the sugar and stir until completely dissolved. Pour over the cabbage.

3. Add the olive oil, mint, salt, and pepper to the bowl. Toss the ingredients to fully incorporate. Cover and place in the refrigerator to marinate, tossing occasionally, for at least 1 hour (overnight is fine). Serve in the Dijon Mustard Pork Chop Sandwiches (page 193). ⟪

»» Smoky Paprika Apple Chips

I first made these chips when working on a guest recipe for my friend Chris Bryant's book Chips. *My contribution there uses* ras el hanout, *a Moroccan spice blend, to flavor the chips. Here, though, it is smoky paprika that imparts a counterbalance to the fruit's sweetness. Plan ahead when making these chips, as they'll need about two and a half hours of bake time before they are crisp enough to serve.* **SERVES 6 TO 8**

YOU WILL NEED

¼ cup sugar

1 tablespoon plus
  1 teaspoon smoky paprika

Nonstick cooking spray
  (I like coconut oil spray)

4 large or 6 medium apples

TO MAKE

1. In a small bowl, combine the sugar and paprika. Set aside.

2. Preheat the oven to 250°F. Line two large baking sheets with parchment paper or silicone baking mats. Spray the paper or baking mats with a generous misting of nonstick cooking spray. Set aside.

3. Wash and dry the apples. Cut ¼ inch off the bottom of each apple. This provides a flat, level surface to place on the mandoline for slicing. Using the mandoline, cut the apple into thin slices, about ⅛ inch thick. If you don't have a mandoline, cut into very thin slices with a large knife. Repeat with the rest of the apples.

4. Once all the apples have been sliced, use a small pointy-tip knife to remove any seeds. Arrange the apple slices in an even layer on the two prepared baking sheets, overlapping the edges of slices as needed.

5. Sprinkle the chips with the paprika sugar. Flip the apple slices and coat on the other side. Rearrange the chips into an even layer.

6. Put the baking sheets into the oven. Bake for 1 hour. Remove the baking sheets from the oven, flip all the chips over, spread them out evenly again, and return to bake for an additional hour. Turn the oven off and leave the baking sheets in the oven for 30 minutes.

7. Remove the baking sheets from the oven. The chips will continue to crisp up as they cool. These are best served the same day they are prepared. «««

»» Pumpkin Whoopie Pies

By definition, a whoopie pie consists of two round, mound-shaped pieces of cake with a sweet filling sandwiched between them. I tend to of think of them as a cupcake in reverse. This version embodies the flavors of autumn: pumpkin, cinnamon, ginger, cloves, and nutmeg. **MAKES 2½ DOZEN**

YOU WILL NEED

for the cookies

2½ cups all-purpose flour

1½ teaspoons sea salt

1½ teaspoons baking powder

1 teaspoon baking soda

1 teaspoon ground cinnamon

½ teaspoon ground ginger

¼ teaspoon ground cloves

1 cup (2 sticks) butter, softened

1½ cups packed light brown sugar

¾ cup granulated sugar

2 eggs, at room temperature
  (see Note)

1¼ cups pure pumpkin puree

2 teaspoons vanilla extract

for the buttercream frosting

3 cups powdered sugar

1 cup (2 sticks) butter,
  at room temperature

2 tablespoons whole milk

1 teaspoon vanilla extract

½ teaspoon ground cinnamon

½ teaspoon ground nutmeg

¼ teaspoon ground ginger

¼ teaspoon ground cloves

TO MAKE

1. *Make the Cookies:* Preheat the oven to 350°F. Line two baking sheets with parchment or silicone baking mats and set aside.

2. In a medium bowl, combine the flour, salt, baking powder, baking soda, cinnamon, ginger, and cloves. Whisk to fully incorporate. Set aside.

3. In a large bowl, beat together the butter, the brown sugar, and the granulated sugar with an electric mixer until pale and light, about 3 to 4 minutes.

4. Add the eggs, one at a time, beating well after each addition. Scrape down the bowl and beaters with a spatula as necessary.

5. Add the pumpkin and vanilla and beat until combined.

6. With the mixer set to low, beat in the flour mixture just until incorporated.

7. Drop the dough by heaping tablespoons 2 inches apart on the prepared baking sheets. Bake for 15 minutes, rotating the pans halfway through. Repeat in order to bake all the batter, which yields slightly more than 4 dozen cookies.

8. Transfer to a cooling rack and allow the cookies to cool fully before spreading with the filling.

9. *Prepare the Filling:* In a large bowl, beat together all the filling ingredients with an electric mixer.

10. *Assemble the Whoopie Pies:* Spread about 2 tablespoons of filling on the bottom of a cookie, and top with another cookie. Repeat until all the cookies have been used.

11. Store in the refrigerator until ready to serve. These are tasty served either at room temperature or chilled.

Note: You can easily bring refrigerated eggs to room temperature by placing them in a bowl of hot tap water for about 10 minutes. «««

»» around the world ««

PICNIC

I have been enthralled with learning how the rest of the world lives for as long as I can recall. In my early twenties, I watched countless foreign films and read a library's worth of international literature. I even toyed with the idea of majoring in anthropology in college before ultimately settling on sociology. Dress, language, habits, etiquette, design, décor, spiritual traditions, terrain, and, of course, foods of cultures the world over have long captivated me.

It wasn't until my late twenties, though, that I finally packed a bag and made it out of the continental United States. That trip, a cruise of the western Caribbean Sea with stops in Key West, Florida; Cozumel, Mexico; and Belize City, Belize, introduced me to weather previously unknown (holy humidity!) and to turquoise waters riddled with fishes, turtles, and coral reefs. It did not, however, give me a keen sense of what it felt like to experience life with the locals, as most of our interactions were short-lived and heavily mediated.

The summer I turned thirty, however, I decided I'd throw caution to the wind, take a risk, and take myself to the United Kingdom for just over a week, which I did. Ten months later and recently married, I honeymooned in continental Europe, spending time in Paris, Monte Carlo, and Rome over the course of two weeks. These trips ignited within me a deep respect for cultural differences and socialized norms and customs. I experienced firsthand just how much context and interpretation and audience matter, when individuals are hoping to communicate and understand one another across cultural divides.

As someone who has long been enamored of cooking and baking, the highlight of these international dalliances, naturally, was the food. A picnic celebrating the culinary traditions of a particular nation or geographic region is a wonderful opportunity to parlay your own international inclinations into something tangible, and delicious. Should the gathering inspire you to book a flight and pack a bag, all the better!

For this picnic, I hosted a "Mediterranean picnic" bash for my husband Glenn's birthday. Because Glenn couldn't decide whether he preferred North African flavors over Greek or Italian ones, we elected to combine them all in one big Mediterranean feast.

✳ to MAKE & DO

SELECT A SITE

The location for this picnic could somehow directly reference the geographic location of the cuisine. If it's for a beach lover, consider holding it surfside. If your guest of honor loves Japan, see if there's a Japanese tea or bonsai garden in your area. Otherwise, anywhere that's beautiful and can be accessed by a wide range of guests of varying ages and abilities is a sure bet.

PLAY GAMES

No matter where in the world you set your compass, games native to that country will be found. At your picnic, consider playing games indigenous to your chosen culture. Whether you're enjoying Greek foods and a rousing game of *Agalmata* ("Statues" in English) or an Indian feast followed by a match of *Kho-Kho* (similar to tag), there's a game for every culinary tradition.

SPECIAL OCCASIONS

An internationally themed picnic is a great idea for a birthday celebration. All manner of celebrations are great opportunities for imbuing a bit of international flair, from bridal showers to graduation parties to anniversaries, baby showers, and housewarmings. If you're hosting, simply determine a beloved cuisine of your guest and build your picnic menu accordingly. This would also be a wonderful way to bring a place "to" a guest of honor, especially a region, country, or city that he or she has always wanted to travel to.

✳ to BEHOLD & EXPLORE

EXPLORE MAPS

Put a map, atlas, or globe in front of me, and I'm content for the next hour. Even if no travel plans are in sight, viewing maps can incite a sense of excitement and adventure. At your picnic, consider putting out maps or atlases of your region of choice. Guests can travel far without ever leaving the comfort of their picnic blanket!

»» Ratatouille

When summer is at its peak and tomatoes, eggplant, peppers, and summer squashes are ripe and abundant, there are few better dishes to prepare than ratatouille. Here I've concentrated the inherent sweetness of tomatoes and eggplant by first roasting them, which also helps to draw out some of the profuse moisture both possess. Pass this recipe on to anyone you know with a backyard garden or simply a fondness for summertime veggies. **SERVES 8 TO 10**

YOU WILL NEED

4 pounds eggplant,
   cut into bite-size pieces

¾ cup plus ⅓ cup olive oil

3 pounds tomatoes,
   cut into wedges

1 large onion, diced

1 red bell pepper, diced

1 yellow or orange bell pepper,
   diced

3 garlic cloves, minced

2 pounds zucchini,
   cut into bite-size pieces

2 pounds yellow squash,
   cut into bite-size pieces

2 tablespoons herbes de Provence

1 tablespoon sea salt

Several grinds of black pepper

A couple dashes of hot sauce

2 tablespoons tomato paste

Fresh herbs, such as parsley,
   marjoram, or thyme leaves,
   for garnish (optional)

TO MAKE

1. Preheat the oven to 400°F. Oil a 9 × 13-inch baking pan and set aside.

2. On a rimmed baking sheet, toss the pieces of eggplant with ½ cup olive oil. On a separate rimmed baking sheet, toss the tomato wedges with ¼ cup olive oil. Place the pans in the oven (tomatoes on higher shelf) and roast for 1 hour.

3. Halfway through the roasting process, add ⅓ cup oil to a stockpot over medium heat and add the onion and bell peppers. Cook, stirring occasionally, until brown around the edges, about 10 to 12 minutes.

4. Add the minced garlic to the stockpot, stir, and sauté for a couple more minutes, and then add the zucchini and yellow squashes. Continue to cook, stirring occasionally, until the eggplant and tomatoes have finished roasting.

5. When the roasted veggies are done, add them to the stockpot. Stir in the herbes de Provence, salt, black pepper, hot sauce, and tomato paste. Cook for 5 more minutes, stirring frequently.

6. Take the pot off the heat. Transfer the veggie mixture into the prepared baking pan. Bake at 400° for 30 minutes.

7. Remove the pan from the oven. Let cool for at least 10 minutes before serving. Garnish with fresh herbs if you like. «««

»» Lamb Stew

This stew is a cornucopia of flavors and aromas. Lamb, dried fruits, herbs, spices, and vegetables are simmered together, resulting in a rich, deep, sweet and savory dish. If you can't find fava beans, lima beans can be substituted. **SERVES 6 TO 8**

YOU WILL NEED

1 tablespoon cumin seeds

1 tablespoon fennel seeds

¼ cup olive oil

2 pounds ground lamb

1 onion, diced

1 red bell pepper, diced

1 yellow or orange bell pepper, diced

3 garlic cloves, minced

2 pounds tomatoes, diced

1¼ cups cooked fava beans

1 tablespoon chopped fresh marjoram

2 teaspoons chopped fresh oregano

1 teaspoon chopped fresh thyme

2 teaspoons sea salt

Several grinds of black pepper

A dash of hot sauce

1 cup wine of your choice

Juice of 1 lemon

2 cups mixed dried fruits, such as raisins, dates, and apricots

Handful of chopped fresh cilantro or parsley

Crumbled feta, to serve (optional)

Hot sauce, to serve (optional)

TO MAKE

1. Toast the cumin and fennel seeds in a dry skillet for 1 to 2 minutes, until fragrant. Set aside.

2. Warm 2 tablespoons of the olive oil in a Dutch oven or stockpot over medium-high heat. Add the ground lamb and sauté, stirring often, until cooked through and starting to brown, about 9 or 10 minutes. Transfer the lamb into a bowl and set aside.

3. Return the empty Dutch oven to the stove top. Add the remaining 2 tablespoons of olive oil and the onion and bell peppers. Sauté until the vegetables are limp and starting to brown, about 10 to 12 minutes.

4. Add the minced garlic and cook for 2 more minutes, stirring frequently. Add the cooked lamb, diced tomatoes, and fava beans. Stir to fully combine.

5. Add the roasted seeds, marjoram, oregano, thyme, salt, black pepper, and hot sauce. Stir to fully incorporate all ingredients.

6. Reduce the heat to low. Simmer for 20 minutes, and then add the wine, lemon juice, and dried fruit.

7. Simmer for 20 minutes more. Turn off the heat, and stir in the cilantro.

8. Serve with crumbled feta and hot sauce, if desired. «‹

Herbed Green Beans *with* Pistachios

Roasting green beans takes them from earthy legumes to robust, browned delights. It's a simple technique that delivers a huge payoff in terms of flavor. Chopped pistachios sprinkled liberally on top add both textural contrast and a welcome bit of saltiness. **SERVES 6 TO 8**

YOU WILL NEED

2 pounds green beans

¼ cup olive oil

1 teaspoon sea salt

Several grinds of black pepper

1 cup white or rosé wine

¼ cup finely chopped roasted and salted pistachios

Juice of 1 lemon

Diced pimento, to serve (optional)

Chopped fresh cilantro or parsley, to serve (optional)

TO MAKE

1. Preheat the oven to 400°F.

2. Prepare the green beans by snapping off both ends of each bean.

3. On a rimmed baking sheet, toss the green beans with the olive oil, salt, and pepper. Space them out evenly and then pour the wine into the pan.

4. Roast for 15 minutes. Using tongs, toss the beans in the pan. Roast for an additional 10 minutes, then remove from the oven.

5. Transfer the roasted green beans to a medium bowl, leaving any remaining wine in the pan.

6. Add the chopped pistachios and lemon juice and toss.

7. Transfer to a lidded container and store in the refrigerator for at least 1 hour; overnight is even better.

8. Garnish with pimento and cilantro when you are ready to serve, if desired. ⋘

Cardamom, Pistachio, *and* Citrus Bundt Cake

I cannot get enough of cardamom. If pistachios and citrus zest are included in the mix, then I've pretty much met my holy trinity of flavors. Fortunately, my husband feels the same. So it was a natural fit with the Mediterranean theme at his picnic to include a birthday cake for him combining these three ingredients. Perfect for a festive occasion such as a birthday, bridal shower, or baby shower, this cake would also be most welcome simply served with a cup of hot coffee for breakfast.

SERVES 12 TO 16

YOU WILL NEED

1 dry bread slice (you can use a piece of toast instead)

⅔ cup roasted and salted pistachios, shelled

2¼ cups all-purpose flour

¼ cup cornstarch

2 teaspoons ground cardamom

1½ teaspoons baking powder

1 teaspoon baking soda

¾ teaspoon sea salt

1 cup (2 sticks) unsalted butter, at room temperature

1½ cups sugar

4 eggs, at room temperature, beaten

2 teaspoons vanilla extract

Zest of 1 orange

Zest of 1 lemon

1 cup whole fat Greek yogurt

TO MAKE

1. Preheat the oven to 350°F. Put the slice of dry bread into a food processor and pulse until fine crumbs form.

2. Next, butter a 10- to 12-cup Bundt pan. Coat the pan with the bread crumbs, and then lightly mist with a nonstick cooking spray (I like to use coconut oil spray). Set aside.

3. Pulse the pistachios briefly in a food processor until finely ground, stopping before they begin to form a paste. Set aside.

4. Scoop 1 cup of all-purpose flour out of its canister or bag and place into a medium bowl. Take 2 tablespoons back out of the bowl and return it to the canister. Repeat with the second cup of flour, adding it to the bowl and then removing 2 tablespoons flour. Measure out ¼ cup of flour and add to the bowl, along with the cornstarch. Using a flour sifter and another bowl, sift the flour/cornstarch blend four times. This process helps to aerate and lighten the flour, essentially creating homemade cake flour.

5. Add the cardamom, baking powder, baking soda, and salt to the flour mixture and whisk to incorporate. Set aside.

6. In a large bowl, beat the butter and sugar together with an electric mixer on medium speed until light and fluffy, about 3 to 4 minutes. Add the beaten eggs and vanilla and beat until well combined, another 3 to 4 minutes. Scrape down the sides of the bowl and the beaters with a spatula. Add the ground pistachios and orange and lemon zest.

continued

7. At a low speed, beat about a third of the flour mixture into the creamed butter mixture. Add half of the yogurt and beat. Add another third of the flour mixture and beat. Then add the remaining yogurt and the remaining flour mixture, beating after each addition. Scrape down the sides of the bowl and the beaters with a spatula, ensuring that all ingredients are fully combined.

8. Pour the batter into the prepared pan and spread out the batter evenly with a spatula. Bake for 50 to 60 minutes, until a knife inserted into the cake comes out clean.

9. Set the pan on a cooling rack and allow to cool completely in the pan. Once cool, loosen the edges gently with a flat knife and then invert the cake onto a serving platter or cake stand. ⫷

»» twilight ««

PICNIC

Most evenings, barring those occasions when heavy cloud cover intervenes, the sky above the forest in which I live becomes downright bewitching. As the sun slowly sets in the west and the last bits of sunlight begin filtering in through cracks in the clouds, things turn rosy for about fifteen to twenty fleeting minutes. That is when the crepuscular light settles in. Stemming from theLatin word *crepusculum*, meaning "twilight," this type of light occurs during dawn and dusk, when the contrasts between light and dark are most stark. Depicted by many a painter illustrating the way the heavens appear to glow rosy and peach as the light fades, the crepuscular light is simply dazzling.

When you work from home full-time as I do, creating a clear delineation between the workday and home and family time is crucial. Otherwise, you're just always working, and that's destined to burn you out, quickly. The way I determine the professional day is done is to watch the light. When I see the shift occurring, the house getting dimmer inside as the scene outside becomes ethereal, I know it's time to close the laptop and step into time with my family. Depending on the time of year and how I'm feeling, I'll brew a cup of tea, crack open a beer, pour a glass of wine, or mix up a cocktail. Often, I'll then slip outside to witness the show in the sky.

In 2006, I took myself to the western highlands of Scotland. Never before have I witnessed such astounding cloud and sunlight interactions. The clouds hung low there at all times of the day, appearing as though they could be touched upon cresting the adjacent sheep-covered hill or knoll. They were big and billowy clouds—playful, even. They weren't stagnant either, instead moving at a brisk pace, as though on their way to some important business or attending to an urgent errand. Things became truly spectacular, though, at sundown. I was there in August, and twilight comes later in the day that time of year. When it came, the sky transformed and the highlands were bathed in warm, rose-tinged light. Never before had I been so awed by the power of twilight. From that point on, I vowed to notice the light more in the late afternoon, and to enjoy and honor its ephemeral qualities.

At this picnic, I wanted to invoke a bit of a wayfaring feeling, as though these picnickers are always on the move, in search of beautiful light. Rugs, fire, and scores of candles work to imbue the scene with comfort, beauty, and a recognition of the profound connection humans have with light and fire in all their incarnations. Warming soup, hearty bread, savory spread, and a cake served right out of its pan speak to relaxed entertaining. All the better for taking in the real star of the evening: the light.

✳ to MAKE & DO

SELECT A SITE

When choosing a location for this picnic, look for an area without much in the way of outdoor lighting. Once the sun starts to set, you want to be able to enjoy the glow of the candles and string lights as much as possible. Outdoor lighting will hinder that, so seek out those spaces that will allow for both enjoying the twilight and viewing the lighting you've provided.

BONFIRE AND CANDLES

Fire is a many splendored thing. It can consume and illuminate, all at once. For this picnic, as the light gently fades, consider surrounding the picnicking site in numerous candles. If the location permits, a bonfire would also be a wonderful addition to the occasion. The flickering glow of flames always captivates, transfixes, and, somehow, soothes. Do be sure to practice fire safety and bring along extra water to extinguish the fire as needed.

✳ to BEHOLD & EXPLORE

STARGAZING

As twilight shifts to evening, the sky will open up with stars (especially if you've selected a picnic site away from the glare of city lights!). Bring along a guidebook, telescope, and/ or knowledgeable stargazer, and look for constellations. This would be especially fun to do on a seasonal basis, picnicking in the same location quarterly and noticing the way in which the heavens shift.

FIREFLY COLLECTING

The annual arrival of fireflies—ephemeral creatures if ever there were ones—is an indicator of warmer days to come. Their lighting is the result of a chemical reaction between the air and an organic compound called luciferin in the fireflies' abdomens. It is done as a mating signal. When the bugs disappear for the season, the upcoming cooler weather is silently heralded. While they're on the go and quickly flashing up the evening, gently collect a few and examine their magical glow.

» Ciorba *de* Perisoare (Romanian Meatball Soup)

When researching the type of soup to serve at this picnic, my husband, Glenn, came across this dish. He contacted his Romanian friend Andrea, asking for pointers and tips. What resulted is a riff on this traditional meatball soup. A base of smoky paprika and tomatoes is enlivened by the inclusion of sauerkraut juice, providing the sour flavor characteristic of Eastern European cuisine. It is refreshing and, owing to the meatballs, hearty and robust, all at once. **SERVES 8 TO 10**

YOU WILL NEED

for the meatballs

1 teaspoon coarse sea salt

3 garlic cloves, minced

3 eggs

1 cup milk

1 tablespoon smoky paprika

1 teaspoon fine sea salt

2 cups fresh bread crumbs

3 pounds ground beef, pork, or lamb (or a combination)

3 tablespoons olive oil

continued

TO MAKE

1. *Prepare the Meatballs:* Chop together the coarse sea salt and the minced garlic (substitute regular sea salt if necessary). Leave to mellow for at least 15 minutes.

2. In a medium bowl, beat the eggs, milk, paprika, and fine salt.

3. Put the bread crumbs into a large bowl. Stir in the egg mixture and let sit for about 1 minute.

4. Add the salted garlic into the bread crumb mixture and stir. Add the ground meat and knead it into the bread crumb mixture until all ingredients are fully incorporated. Roll the mixture into balls the size of Ping-Pong balls.

5. In a large stockpot or Dutch oven, heat about 1 tablespoon of the olive oil over medium-high heat. In three or four batches, cook the meatballs until mostly brown all around, about 6 to 8 minutes per batch, adding the rest of the olive oil as needed.

6. Drain the meatballs on paper towels. Transfer to a bowl and set aside while you make the soup.

continued

for the soup

1 medium onion, diced

2 carrots, diced

1 celeriac, peeled and diced

1 tablespoon caraway seed

1 tablespoon celery seed

3 garlic cloves, minced

¼ cup tomato paste

4 cups crushed tomatoes
(canned is fine—home-canned
is even better!)

2 quarts beef stock

1 cup sauerkraut juice

2 tablespoons white wine vinegar

1 tablespoon paprika
(smoky or hot, depending
on preference)

1 tablespoon sugar

1 teaspoon sea salt

1 cup chopped fresh lovage,
celery leaves, or parsley
(or a combination)

Sour cream, to serve

Crusty bread, to serve

7. *Make the Soup:* After the meatballs are done, leave about 3 tablespoons of oil in the stockpot and place over medium-high heat. Add the onion, carrots, and celeriac and sauté, stirring frequently, until cooked through and lightly browned around the edges, about 20 minutes.

8. Add the caraway seeds, celery seeds, and minced garlic and continue to cook, stirring, for 2 minutes.

9. Add the cooked meatballs and tomato paste and gently stir for 1 minute. Add the tomatoes, stock, sauerkraut juice, vinegar, paprika, sugar, and salt. Reduce the heat to low and simmer, stirring occasionally, until slightly reduced, about 45 minutes.

10. Turn off the heat and stir in the chopped herbs. Adjust salt to taste.

11. Serve with good bread and with sour cream on the side. ⋘

Smoky Cauliflower Spread

Cauliflower doesn't get enough love, in my book. Often served barely steamed and hardly edible as a side-dish afterthought, it's a delicious vegetable that needs to have its day in the sun, and that day is today! Roasted, the florets develop a wonderful sweetness and tenderness. Cream cheese, sour cream, and paprika aid in taking things from ho-hum to hallelujah! **MAKES 5 TO 6 CUPS**

YOU WILL NEED

2 cauliflower heads

½ cup olive oil

1 cup cream cheese, at room temperature

1 cup sour cream

2 teaspoons smoked sea salt (plain is fine too)

1 tablespoon smoky paprika

Juice of 1 lemon

Crusty bread, to serve

TO MAKE

1. Preheat the oven to 450°F.

2. Break the cauliflower heads down into florets. Put on a rimmed baking sheet and toss with ¼ cup of the olive oil. Roast in the oven for 40 minutes, until browned around the edges.

3. Remove the pan from the oven and let cool for a few minutes. While still warm, transfer the cauliflower to a food processor and puree. Add the cream cheese and process until incorporated. Add the sour cream, salt, paprika, and lemon juice and puree.

4. Serve with bread, at room temperature or lightly chilled. «

Fig *and* Orange Skillet Cake

I love skillet cakes. Served right out of the pan, they transfer seamlessly from the oven to the serving table—no extra cleanup necessary. Figs, oranges, and cinnamon form a flavorful holy trinity. Perfect for dessert, any leftovers are equally sublime for breakfast or at teatime. **MAKES ONE 12-INCH SKILLET CAKE**

YOU WILL NEED

2 cups all-purpose flour

1 teaspoon baking powder

1 teaspoon ground cinnamon

½ teaspoon baking soda

½ teaspoon sea salt

½ cup (1 stick) unsalted butter, softened

1 cup sugar

2 eggs, at room temperature (see Note)

Zest and juice of 1 orange

1 teaspoon vanilla extract

¾ cup Greek yogurt

1 pint small fresh figs, cut in half

¼ cup turbinado sugar

TO MAKE

1. Preheat the oven to 375°F. Liberally butter a 12-inch cast iron skillet and set aside.

2. In a small bowl, whisk together the flour, baking powder, cinnamon, baking soda, and salt.

3. In a large bowl, beat the butter and regular sugar with an electric mixer until pale and fluffy, about 3 to 4 minutes.

4. Add the eggs to the creamed butter one at a time, beating well after each addition. Scrape down the bowl and beaters with a spatula as necessary.

5. Add the orange zest and juice and the vanilla extract and beat until thoroughly combined.

6. With the mixer set to low, add half of the flour mixture and beat until just incorporated. Beat in the yogurt, then add the remaining half of the flour mixture and beat until just combined.

7. Pour the batter into the prepared pan, distributing it evenly. Press the fig halves partway into the batter, cut sides up, until they are even with the batter. Sprinkle the turbinado sugar evenly over the surface of the batter.

8. Bake for 30 to 35 minutes, until the top is golden and a knife inserted into the center comes out clean. Let cool at least 15 minutes before serving from the pan.

Note: You can easily bring refrigerated eggs to room temperature by placing them in a bowl of hot tap water for about 10 minutes. «<

» winter «

PICNIC

Several years ago, I read a humorous take on the twelve astrological signs regarding what a person representing each might bring to a potluck or how they might behave at one. While the Gemini (my husband) would show up with six dishes because he couldn't whittle his selections down to one, and the Virgo (my father) would bring a poached salmon that he'd caught himself—naturally—the Cancer (me) would simply leave the potluck early because it wasn't held at her house. I laughed and laughed when I read this, because it is so incredibly true.

It can be difficult to get me to leave my house and property. I am the ultimate homebody. At no other time of the year is this more especially true than during the winter months. I am fond of winter in the way that many people typically are of summer. Where they pine for bathing suits, flip-flops, and ice cream, I long for wool sweaters, shearling slippers, and mugs of cocoa. I'll trade in watermelon for a hot pot roast any day. You can keep your air-conditioning, thank you—I prefer to feed firewood to my woodstove.

My favorite part of winter is actually the being-at-home aspect of it. Cozying up indoors, in comfortable clothing, with minimal daylight hours and soothing beverages, is truly a balm to my soul. Close friends of mine cringe and wince at the first frost date in the forecast, while I breathe deeper and feel a massive pang of excitement and anticipation.

While staying comfy by the fire, slowly cooking a stew or soup all day, is a major part of winter's charm for me, I also very much look forward to getting outside. Whenever snow falls, a somewhat irregular and sporadic occurrence here in the mountains of western North Carolina, all else gets put aside. We gear up in snow boots and gloves, snow pants and scarves, and collect the sled for mischief and merriment out in the snow and ice.

A winter picnic is a wonderful opportunity to make the most of the time of year that is typically associated with staying indoors entirely. Warming foods, inspiring activities, and playful exploration of the frozen setting can work wonders to thaw hearts, minds, and fingertips!

SELECT A SITE

This picnic begs for snow. In fact, it's necessary for some of the activities and is truly the highlight of the event. After that prerequisite is fulfilled, you can site this picnic pretty much anywhere snow is present. A backyard would be the most accessible location, of course, and require the least amount of snow-underfoot-schlepping, but a park, ski area, forest, or frozen lake would be equally lovely to picnic at.

SNOW PAINTING

While a blanket of white snow over everything in view is a lovely sight to behold, how about injecting a bit of vibrant color into the scene? Snow painting can be as easy as adding food coloring to spray bottles.

Simply fill several spray bottles with cold water. Next, add several drops of food coloring to each bottle until you've achieved whatever colors you prefer. Head outdoors and use the snow as your canvas!

FROZEN BUBBLES

On especially chilly days, it's possible to create frozen bubbles. The crystalline patterns that develop on their surfaces are beautiful to watch forming. Whenever the temperature drops below freezing, head outdoors with some bubble liquid and a bubble wand (of any size, but larger wands will create some of the most spectacular frozen bubbles).

Dip the wand into the liquid. Slowly, carefully, wave your wand until a bubble forms, and then quickly catch it with the wand. Within just a bit of time, it will freeze briefly and then shatter. The amount of time it takes your bubble to freeze is based on both the size of the bubble and the outdoor temperatures.

✳ *to* BEHOLD & EXPLORE

SNOWFLAKE EXAMINATION

It's true: no two snowflakes are the same (but they do tend to be six-sided). Kind of amazing, when you consider the millions of flakes necessary to blanket the landscape. Bring along a magnifying glass on your picnic, as well as a small glass plate. If it's snowing, place the plate on the ground to collect some falling flakes. Otherwise, scoop a small bit of snow up with the plate, about a teaspoon or less. Use your magnifying lens to examine the shapes, including prisms, columns, stars, hexagonal plates, needles, dendrites, and many more. You can look up www.snowcrystals.com on your smartphone for on-site identification, or bring along a snowflake-identification book with you.

WINTER BOTANICALS

I recall long ago reading an article in a gardening magazine that encouraged planting items that will offer "winter interest." While many plants bloom, flower, and then die back for the winter, others hold on to their stems and branches, creating platforms for holding snow or ice. Others even flower in the winter. Such objects serve to break up an otherwise uniform landscape. See what sorts of winter botanicals are on view wherever you choose to picnic.

to savor & sip

⟫ Karelian Hot Pot

Named after Karelia, a remote region of Finland that borders Russia, this filling stew combines three types of meat with carrots, potatoes, and aromatics. For a winter picnic, I can think of fewer locations better qualified to create warming foods that are so essential when the mercury plunges. This is traditionally served with lingonberry jam, but because that's not readily available for many of us, I'm offering a recipe for a homemade alternative: cranberry preserves. Add some rye toast and dill pickle spears, and you've got a dish as flavorful as it is satiating on a cold winter's day.

SERVES 8 TO 10

YOU WILL NEED

2 tablespoons olive oil

2 pounds beef stew meat

2 pounds pork stew meat

1 pound lamb stew meat

1 large onion, coarsely chopped

2 carrots, peeled and cut into disks

3 cups beef stock, plus
    an additional 1–2 cups

2 teaspoons sea salt

1 teaspoon black peppercorns

1 teaspoon allspice berries

3 bay leaves

2 pounds small, medium-starch
    potatoes, cut into bite-size
    pieces

Cranberry, Ginger, and Orange
    Preserves (page 230), to serve

Slices of rye toast, to serve

Dill pickle spears, to serve

TO MAKE

1. In an oven-safe stockpot or Dutch oven, warm the olive oil over medium-high heat. Add the stew meat, and cook until evenly browned, about 15 minutes, turning the meat pieces as needed. Meanwhile, preheat the oven to 300°F.

2. Add the onion, carrots, stock, salt, pepper, allspice, and bay leaves to the meat and stir. Cook for 5 minutes, then transfer the uncovered pot into the oven.

3. Bake for 3 hours, giving the pot a quick stir every 45 minutes or so. Check the liquid level. If it has reduced by half or more, add 1 to 2 additional cups of stock, as needed. Add the potatoes and stir to incorporate into the meat. Bake, stirring every 10 minutes, for about 1 more hour, until the potatoes are cooked through.

4. Serve with Cranberry, Ginger, and Orange Preserves on rye toast with dill pickles.

Note: Any combination of stew meats can be used, so long as the total is 5 pounds. ⟪

»» Cranberry, Ginger, *and* Orange Preserves

Tart cranberries offer a vibrant, lively foil to the stew's umami flavors. Ginger imparts a bit of heat and warmth while orange zest further brightens the preserve. Slather this generously atop rye toast to accompany the Karelian Hot Pot (page 229). **MAKES 3 CUPS**

YOU WILL NEED

3 cups cranberries

1½ cups sugar

1½ cups water

1 tablespoon grated fresh ginger

1 tablespoon freshly grated
  orange zest

TO MAKE

1. Rinse the cranberries under cool water and set aside.

2. In a large, heavy stainless steel saucepan, combine the sugar and water. Bring to a boil over medium-high heat, then reduce the heat to medium and boil until the sugar is completely dissolved, about 5 minutes.

3. Add the cranberries. Simmer, stirring occasionally to prevent sticking, until the berries have burst, about 12 minutes. Add the ginger and orange zest and cook for an additional 5 minutes. Remove the pan from the heat.

4. Let cool, then transfer to a lidded container and store in the refrigerator until serving. Leftover portions can be stored, refrigerated, for up to 2 or 3 weeks. «««

»» S'Mores Brownies

While fireside s'mores are a summertime staple, S'Mores Brownies are what I want come winter. A prebaked graham cracker crust is the foundation for a fudgy, rich center topped off with melted, browned marshmallows. Do be sure to give the pan plenty of time to cool before attempting to slice into brownies. This will allow for clean cuts; otherwise, the marshmallows will tug and tear.

SERVES 12 TO 16

YOU WILL NEED

for the crust

2 cups crushed graham crackers

1 cup (2 sticks) unsalted butter, melted

½ teaspoon sea salt

for the filling

1 cup all-purpose flour

½ teaspoon sea salt

1 cup (2 sticks) unsalted butter

½ cup dark cocoa powder (65% cocoa content or higher)

¾ cup chopped dark chocolate (65% cocoa content or higher)

4 eggs

1½ cups sugar

½ cup packed light brown sugar

2 teaspoons vanilla extract

Large marshmallows (approximately a 7-ounce bag)

TO MAKE

1. *Prepare the Crust:* Preheat the oven to 350°F. Spray a 9 × 13-inch baking pan with nonstick cooking spray or generously butter the bottom and sides. Set aside.

2. In a medium bowl, combine the graham crackers, melted butter, and salt. Stir with a wooden spoon until the butter is fully incorporated.

3. Transfer the mixture to the prepared baking pan and press firmly with your hands, evenly covering the bottom of the pan. Bake for 10 minutes. Set aside to cool while you make the brownie filling.

4. *Prepare the Filling:* Combine the flour and salt in a medium bowl and set aside.

5. Cover the bottom of a medium stockpot with 2 inches of water. Rest a large metal bowl on the rim of the pot to create a double boiler. Put the butter, cocoa powder, and chocolate pieces into the metal bowl and bring the water to a boil. Gently stir the chocolate mixture until everything is fully melted and incorporated. Remove the bowl and set aside to cool slightly.

6. In a medium bowl, beat the eggs, sugar, brown sugar, and vanilla with an electric mixer until pale and creamy, about 3 to 4 minutes.

7. Gradually beat the chocolate mixture into the egg mixture. Add the flour mixture and beat until everything is just incorporated, stopping to scrape down the beaters and bowl with a spatula as necessary.

continued

8. *Assemble the Brownies:* Pour the chocolate filling over the prepared graham cracker crust. Top with enough marshmallows placed on their sides to just about cover the surface—it's alright if chocolate filling peeks through here and there.

9. Bake for 30 to 35 minutes, until the marshmallows are browned and a knife inserted into the filling comes out clean. Allow to cool completely before cutting. To help slice through the gooey marshmallows, fill a glass with very hot water, then dip the knife into the water before making the first cut. Wipe the knife clean with a paper towel and dip it into the water again before every subsequent cut. ⫷⫷⫷

»index

ABOUT THE
» *photographer*

Jen Altman is a photographer and writer. Her work has been exhibited throughout North America and is held in private collections across the globe. Her clients include Chronicle Books and *Martha Stewart Living*, *Food & Wine*, and *Kinfolk* magazines, among others. Jen is the author of *Instant Love: How to Make Magic and Memories with Polaroids* with Susannah Conway and Amanda Gilligan, *Gem and Stone: Jewels of Earth, Sea, and Sky*, and *Photographing Your Children: A Handbook of Style and Instruction*. Jen lives in Asheville, North Carolina. You can follow her adventures in food and travel at her acclaimed blog, *Nectar*.

Tim Robison

ABOUT THE
» *author*

Ashley English has degrees in holistic nutrition and sociology. She has worked over the years with a number of nonprofit organizations committed to social and agricultural issues, is a member of Slow Food USA, and writes a regular column for the quarterly publication *Taproot*. She is the author of four books in the Homemade Living series (*Canning and Preserving*, *Keeping Chickens*, *Keeping Bees*, *Home Dairy*), as well as *A Year of Pies*, *Handmade Gatherings*, and *Quench*. Ashley and her family live in Candler, North Carolina, where they are converting their land into a thriving homestead. Follow their adventures at www.smallmeasure.com.